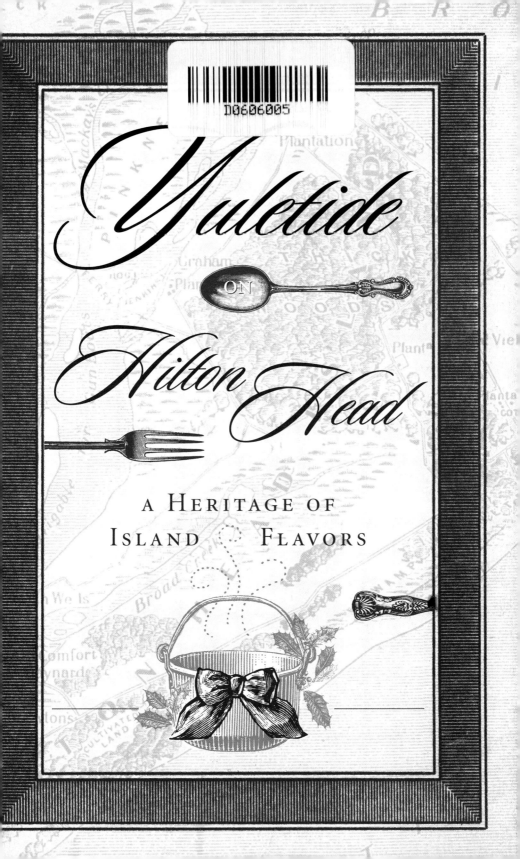

Yuletide

ON

Hilton Head

A Heritage of
Island Flavors

Yuletide on Hilton Head
A Heritage of Island Flavors

Published by
Yuletide Publishing Committee Inc.
PO Box 22961
Hilton Head Island
SC 29925

All profits generated from the sale of this book will be distributed
to thirty-two regional health and human services agencies.
The publisher would like to thank United Way of Beaufort County Inc.
for their role in making this distribution possible.

First Printing 1999

International Standard Book Number
0-9664986-0-7

Library of Congress Card Catalog Number 98-060971

Many recipes in this book
have been handed down through generations
and adapted over time
to reflect changing tastes and ingredient availability.
Consistent with this, all recipes have been tested
and some further modified.
Although the selections herein reflect
the favorites of both contributors and the Culinary Editors
no claims are made with respect to their originality.

Design by Sandra Murray Design
San Francisco,
California

Typesetting by Curry Printing, Hilton Head Island, SC

Back Cover Watercolor by Island Artist Brenda Weiss
Cover background map, 1861,
courtesy of the Coastal Discovery Museum
Cover liners, GW&CB Colton, 1877

Printed in the USA by
Cookbook Resources
Dallas, Texas

FOREWORD

This cookbook was born of nostalgia. To understand the motivation for this book, it is important to appreciate the spirit behind it all. I believe it is best expressed in this quote from an anonymous essay given to us by Kathy Cox, "The Yule Story":

> *'Yule' is a word from one of the most ancient tongues. It is related to words like yell, and yodel! It means to call out in song. But the first beings had never heard a song. So they sought the Moon's advice. "How shall we Yule?" they asked. "How shall we sing a song?"*
>
> *"Take the best of what you have, of what you are, take what you love and cherish most. Take your joys, dreams, and fondest hopes, and weave them all together in a sound." And so they did.*
>
> *They climbed the tallest trees, hills and mountains. They stood in all the places that would bring them closest to the Sun. They shut their eyes and thought the best of thoughts and feelings, and dreamt the first dreams.*
>
> *As they did, their voices rang and made a bridge of song across the sky to reach the distant Sun. Sun heard and turned, smiled, and wrapped himself in all of his light and warmth and sped to where the Yuleing voices called. As he drew near, the sleeping Earth did stir, and dreamt a dream of spring. The wheel of life made its first round. Hope and love prevailed. Ever since, that time of year has been called 'Yule' in honor of the first song.*

When we celebrate Yule nowadays — with 'hope and love prevailing' — our thoughts invariably turn to the pleasure and gratification that accompanies festive cooking and sharing our holiday tables.

In 1996, the Hilton Head ISLAND PACKET publicized a recipe contest in conjunction with an annual musical event, "Yuletide: A Celebration of Christmas Through the Ages." The recipes submitted during that contest became the genesis of this book.

In the hands of our talented and enthusiastic editors, and through the generosity of many good friends who wished to be a part of this endeavor, the content and richness of the book has grown beyond our initial dream.

Thus, **YULETIDE ON HILTON HEAD ~ *A Heritage of Island Flavors,*** a very special cookbook representing the many cultures, origins and culinary customs of our diverse island community, has become a reality. Just as the traditional "Yuletide Celebration" is a festival of music and song, those who have worked on this book feel that it too sings a song ... a song of satisfaction and pleasure, of love and of fun. We hope it also sings for you.

Jane Plante
Honorary Patron
Yuletide Publishing Committee, Inc.

DEDICATION

The Editors dedicate this book to the good cooks everywhere
whose culinary curiosity,
insatiable appetite for knowledge
and pursuit of new ideas,
have made cooking one of life's greatest pleasures.

To Claudia - my dear friend,
what sweet 'moments' we share over these
many years of friendship -- and it all started
over our passion for good food. I treasure
every one of them. I can't think of anyone I'd
rather share this first
cookbook of mine with
than you. You are rare,
dear Claudia.
Love,
Dotti

(handwritten signatures)

4/9/99

ACKNOWLEDGEMENTS

The Editors wish to thank Jane Plante for her inspiration and persuasion, and all those
who contributed their favorite recipes for consideration in our book (see page 274).

'Yuletide' is also indebted to our graphic designer who has given so much of her time
and talent to the creation of this publication. As well, we must acknowledge the
significant contribution of The Yuletide Publishing Committee, chaired by Ian Murray, our
wine enthusiast, and supported by the Editors plus George De Salvio and Sally Christy.

Special thanks are due as well, to Joe Carty, Bill Smoot and Bill Littell for their
invaluable assistance, and to Brenda Weiss for her "Santa's Trawler" Yuletide watercolor
(back cover) from her Bluffton Gallery. Finally thanks are due to the many others who
will continue, well after publication, to contribute their efforts in support of this
cookbook for the benefit of our Beaufort County health and human service agencies.

(THE EDITORS AT WORK)

STIRRING THE CHRISTMAS PUDDING.

Engraving by Henry Woods, Harper's Weekly December 10, 1881

ABOUT THE EDITORS

Creating "Yuletide" has been a labor of love and pure gastronomic pleasure by four of Hilton Head's best known culinary professionals. It eloquently and colorfully reflects, through their significant recipe and editorial input, their pride and commitment to both their profession and their Island home. They are all members of the International Association of Culinary Professionals, the James Beard Foundation, and the American Southern Food Institute.

Dotti Trivison, a national food judge and lifelong food journalist, brought her enthusiasm and expertise to the ISLAND PACKET 10 years ago. The many newspapers going out of state on Wednesdays are usually going to those who don't want to miss a single issue of the Packet's outstanding Food Section which Dotti writes.

Phyllis White, like many, vacationed on Hilton Head Island long before she became a year-round resident. She established the first professional cooking school on the Island and eagerly volunteers her boundless energy to food related events. She now operates her popular Cooking School of Hilton Head Island programs in affiliation with Main Street Inn.

Mary Murray brought to Hilton Head Island a vast knowledge of the food world from her entrepreneurial experiences as cooking school owner, restaurateur, and fine food and specialty cookware retailer. She continues to use her overflow of ideas and culinary expertise as a partner in *Cuisine~Cuisine*, developing recipes and teaching private cooking classes.

Marion Conlin came to Hilton Head Island via Minneapolis where she was well known as a culinary educator, cookbook author, and for her tours of European cooking schools, markets, and vineyards. Known on the Island for her popular cooking class series, "Men in the Kitchen", she is also a partner in *Cuisine~Cuisine* and engaged in numerous writing projects.

TABLE OF CONTENTS

"Our Heritage of Flavors"
Island vignettes precede each chapter

*Appetizing Island starters that set high standards
for any Yuletide event.*

*Favorite beginnings, colorful accents, and Island flavors:
perfect for seasonal menu planning.*

*These entrées, whether new or traditional, Lowcountry or
international, all say "special occasion."*

*Complement the main event the Hilton Head way,
with a burst of holiday color and seasonings.*

*It's not Yuletide without them, from biscotti, chutney
and salsa, to sorbets, egg nog and punch!*

Islanders' Favorite Finales

To appeal to the sweet tooth in us all, simple holiday favorites and tempting decadent creations.

Yuletide Mornings

Breads, breakfasts and brunches … wake up and warm up with an international flair.

The Christmas Cookie Jar

Cookies fill us with the spirit of Christmas when the cookie jar becomes the heart of the kitchen.

Kids in the Kitchen

Recipes kids love to make, when they star as 'chef du jour' on Hilton Head.

The Spirit of Giving

Nothing says "thank you" better than a gift from a Lowcountry kitchen.

Very Merry Menus

Fourteen menus for entertaining from the Yuletide collection, complete with timely holiday libations.

INTRODUCTION

Yuletide! Of all the seasons that mark our passage through the year, the Yuletide season carries the greatest meaning. It is a time for memories, for sharing, for giving thanks, for celebrating, and for gathering in our homes with family and friends.

YULETIDE ON HILTON HEAD ~ A Heritage of Island Flavors, is a cookbook of tradition. It is also a cookbook that celebrates the love of the Lowcountry. It exemplifies the traditional festive best of many of our good cooks, reflecting both their origins and their assimilation. It is also contemporary and about today.

It is a collection of irresistible family recipes brought to the Carolina Lowcountry by colonizers from all fifty states and from abroad. Hilton Head is truly a melting pot. We play host to visitors from around the world. It's the international flair that makes living on this barrier island so enjoyable.

Originally, the Island was inhabited by native Americans who were hunters and fishermen. Then came 30,000 Union troops, plantation owners, and the Gullah culture. In time, the Island became the domain of 20th century lumbering interests.

It was not until the mid-fifties that the dream of visionary Charles Fraser became a reality. His desire to develop this small barrier island as a haven for those committed to respecting its natural beauty and rich environmental culture, has become a much respected international model.

As the Island developed, it brought a diverse population from all parts of the country and overseas. With them came their traditions as passed on to them by friends and neighbors, aunts, mothers, grandmothers, and great grandmothers. Immediately, wonderful food became a top priority and remains an integral part of our daily lives.

In setting our Yuletide tables, Islanders have lovingly adapted many of their traditional recipes to include the culinary wealth of the Lowcountry, rich farm lands, abundant game, and seafoods. It offers a delightful array of local products from native oysters, shrimp, and blue crabs to a wide variety of fresh produce, which reflects its two growing seasons each year. In fact, as a welcome mat to the Island, you are greeted not only by open trucks featuring fresh local shrimp but

also by rustic roadside stands, decked-out with colorful umbrellas covering baskets of fruit and produce, and displaying hastily prepared homemade signs offering "Peaches, Tomatoes, and Vidalia Onions."

In YULETIDE ON HILTON HEAD you will find a recipe for Pioneer Dressing from a Missouri transplant whose great-grandmother brought the recipe along while crossing the plains in a Conestoga heading for Utah. A ninety-two year old sent her recipe for Mallow Date-Nut Roll. Then there are Coconut Mincemeat Bars from a bakery on the Jersey shore, a Tourtière which is traditionally served in French Canada on New Year's Eve, and a long standing ISLAND PACKET favorite, Christmas Eve Oyster Corn Chowder.

Lowcountry influences show in succulent Plantation Style Seafood Gumbo using seafood from our native waters and okra from our fields, Gullah Yam and Peanut Soup, St. Helena's Stew of Blackeyed Peas and Ham, Scalloped Bluffton Oysters, and Moss Creek Pecan Pie with Bourbon Cream.

All recipes have been tested and updated by the editors. They have been redesigned for modern cooks with a modern timetable, and are as big in flavor as they are in history.

When summer visitors leave this little resort Island our community becomes relatively quiet. Then the pace picks up again during Yuletide which we celebrate from Thanksgiving through New Year's Day. There is much merriment ... festive lighting, tree trimming, art, ballet, theater, musical celebrations, black-tie charity balls, holiday parties ... and Santa arrives in a sailboat!

It is especially during Yuletide that we revive those family heirloom recipes that have been treasured from generation to generation. The kitchen once again becomes the heart of the home where so many wonderful holiday memories are formed. It is a joy to share Hilton Head's favorite recipes with you ... they are our genuine "heritage of flavors."

Dotti Trivison
Food Writer,
The Island Packet

FROM CULINARY ROOTS

Southern cooking is the food of her regions. What is available where you live in the South, what your ancestors prepared before you, is the real food.

Southern cooking embraces soul food, which is a blend of African and native American; Creole, which is a marriage of Spanish and French; foods from Floridians who drew from the Caribbean; and the cooking of the southwest with its strong Mexican overtones and barbecues.

On Hilton Head we're known as the Lowcountry. Our sandy soil was once ocean floor. There are more than 5,000 acres of wetlands, salt marshes, rivers, swamps, ponds, creeks, lagoons and former rice fields. It's the land of alligators, deer and birds.

It's the land of the Geeches and the Gullahs – their influence is at the heart of the real Lowcountry cooking. Lowcountry food is Creole cooking, but more heavily influenced by Africans than is the cuisine of Louisiana. Country French traditions abound, but soups in the Lowcountry might contain okra, and water in which rice was cooked as thickeners rather than a roux.

The tides that flow in and out of our vast marshlands bring meaty, juicy, salty oysters. They are continually washed by the incredible flow of our eight-foot tide, one of the largest on the East coast of America. Shrimp fill our creeks, and clams and blue crabs are abundant.

Frogmore stew and barbecue, fish frys, oyster roasts, shrimp boils, light crab cakes that are practically all crab, catfish stews, she crab soups, tiny butter beans, boiled green peanuts, benne crackers, hush puppies, pilau, Hoppin' John, and stone-ground grits – that's Lowcountry!

A Lowcountry meal is seldom a series of courses, but a sideboard brimming with offerings from soup to nuts. The food itself is the entertainment. Though few of us today were born here, most of us live here by choice and are passionate about our region. We share with you our culinary heritage and our flavors.

FIRSTS & FOREMOSTS

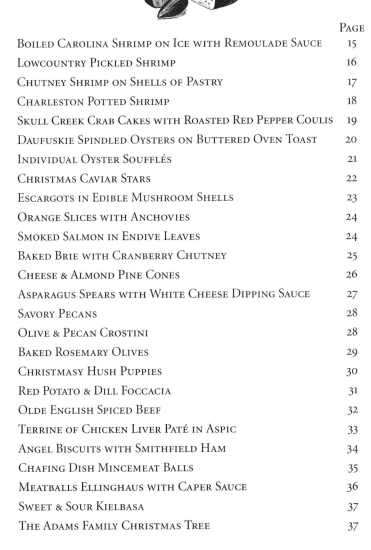

page 13

Enjoy the holidays and indulge yourself!

This collection of 'openers'

invites and appeals.

Each is a slightly exotic

and totally delightful version of someone's favorite.

Appetizers can range from

just a bite on your way out,

to setting the stage for a theme dinner.

They also work well as a thoughtfully chosen

collection for a cocktail buffet.

BOILED CAROLINA
SHRIMP ON ICE
WITH REMOULADE SAUCE

2 tablespoons Old Bay seasoning
1 lemon cut in half
2 pounds jumbo Carolina shrimp in the shell
Large bowl of crushed ice
1 or 2 lemons, quartered

Fill a large non-reactive pot with water; bring to boil.
Add seasoning and lemon. Drop shrimp into boiling
water. As soon as water returns to boil, and shrimp have
turned pink, drain in large colander.

Cover colander with a kitchen towel and allow shrimp
to cool before chilling in refrigerator.

At serving time peel the shrimp, leaving tails intact. Fill
a large bowl with crushed ice and pile shrimp on top.
Garnish with lemon wedges.

Serve with Remoulade Sauce or favorite cocktail sauce.
Yield: 8 appetizer servings

Carolina shrimp have very thin shells. When prepared by this uniquely Carolina method they are particularly tender. This method works with other varieties of shrimp, as well.

Remoulade Sauce
2 teaspoons chopped fresh tarragon
1 tablespoon chopped fresh parsley
1 teaspoon capers, drained, and chopped
1/2 teaspoon anchovy paste
1 teaspoon ketchup
1 tablespoon Dijon or Creole mustard
3/4 cup mayonnaise

Combine all ingredients and stir until well blended. Let
stand 1 hour before serving. Keeps up to 2 weeks,
covered, in refrigerator.

LOWCOUNTRY
PICKLED SHRIMP

1/4 cup vegetable oil
3 cloves garlic, minced
1 cup diced onions
2 pounds shrimp, poached, shelled, and deveined
3 small onions thinly sliced and separated into rings
3/4 cup olive oil
3/4 cup white wine vinegar
1/2 teaspoon dry vermouth
1 1/2 teaspoons salt
Generous grind of black pepper
1/4 teaspoon dry mustard
1/4 teaspoon chili powder
1 teaspoon finely minced parsley

Heat oil in large sauté pan. Add garlic and diced onions; sauté 5 minutes or until translucent. Add shrimp; sauté 3 to 4 minutes. Remove from heat and cool completely.

Combine remaining ingredients and add to shrimp mixture. Place in glass bowl; marinate, covered, 24 hours. Serve slightly chilled, just above room temperature, with thinly sliced rounds of crusty French bread.
Yield: 8 servings

CHUTNEY SHRIMP
ON SHELLS OF PASTRY

1 recipe for single 10-inch pie crust or from the
grocery freezer case
6 (4 to 5-inch) extra deep scallop shells
1/2 cup chopped onion
1/4 cup butter
2 1/2 cup chopped onion
1/4 cup butter
2 1/2 teaspoons curry powder, or to taste
1/3 cup chopped mango chutney
3 cups shelled, deveined small shrimp, cooked
1 finely chopped hard-cooked egg
3 tablespoons minced parsley

Preheat oven to 375 degrees. Prepare a favorite pie
crust recipe or unroll a pastry sheet from the grocery.
Roll pastry 1/8 inch thick on lightly floured surface.
Oil six scallop shells and line each with pastry,
trimming edges with dull knife. Gently press pastry
against each shell so all indentations will be
imprinted in the pastry and weight down with dried
beans or rice. Bake on middle rack about 10 minutes,
or until pastry shells are golden. Allow to cool before
removing pastry from shells.

To make the filling of 'Chutney Shrimp,' sauté onion
in butter until golden. Stir in curry powder and
chutney; mix well. Add shrimp, tossing until well
coated with sauce and heated through. Do not allow
to boil. Spoon evenly onto pastry shells. Sprinkle with
egg and parsley.
Yield: 6 servings

*Get your gala holiday
dinner off to an
auspicious start
with Chutney Shrimp
attractively served in
individual pastries
in the form of
scallop shells.*

CHARLESTON POTTED SHRIMP

1 pound (150 to 225 count) frozen cooked cocktail shrimp
1/2 pound butter
Dash Tabasco sauce
2 teaspoons fresh lemon juice
1 teaspoon mild curry powder
Snipped chives, or finely minced parsley, for garnish

Potted shrimp is a mainstay of Lowcountry entertaining. Charlestonians call it shrimp paste. Either way, rich curry butter with a trace of lemon and a hint of Tabasco brings out the flavors of our local shrimp. Fresh exotic spices for creating curry-blends have come through the nearby port of Charleston since colonial days.

Thaw shrimp overnight in refrigerator. (Do not thaw in water.) Next day, drain and blot dry.

Melt butter in saucepan over moderate heat. Skim foam from top and pour clear butter into side dish leaving behind the milk solids. Discard milk solids, and return butter to saucepan.

Add shrimp to butter and place over moderate heat. Add Tabasco, lemon juice, and curry powder. Simmer shrimp for about 1 minute. Cool slightly. Transfer to bowl of food processor. Pulse processor 4 or 5 times roughly chopping the shrimp (do not purée). Taste, and sharpen flavors by addition of lemon juice, curry, or Tabasco if needed. Spoon into three 6-ounce ramekins. Cover with plastic wrap and chill for several hours.

To serve, garnish lightly with chives or parsley and place ramekin in center of serving plate. Surround with toast rounds. If serving for tea, spoon small amounts onto toast rounds or sandwich between thinly sliced white bread.

Yield: 3 (6-ounce) ramekins or
4 dozen tea sandwiches

SKULL CREEK CRAB CAKES
WITH ROASTED RED PEPPER COULIS

Skull Creek Crab Cakes
1 cup finely chopped Vidalia onion
3 tablespoons finely chopped green pepper
3 tablespoons finely chopped red pepper
2 tablespoons butter
2 pounds fresh crab meat
2 tablespoons Worcestershire sauce
1 teaspoon fresh lemon juice
1 cup fresh bread crumbs
4 eggs, lightly beaten
1 teaspoon salt
White pepper, to taste
Flour for dusting
Butter sufficient for sautéing crab cakes

Sauté onion and peppers in butter until onions are transparent. Mix together with remaining seasoning ingredients (except flour and butter). Toss gently to prevent breaking up crab meat. Form into 12 patties for first course servings (or 24 miniature patties for appetizer servings). Dust crab cakes lightly with flour and sauté in butter until crisp crust is formed.
Yield: 12 first course servings or 24 appetizer servings

Roasted Red Pepper Coulis
4 red bell peppers
2 cloves garlic, minced
1/2 teaspoon fresh thyme leaves
1/4 cup extra virgin olive oil
Salt and fresh ground black pepper, to taste

Roast peppers over open flame (or under broiler) until skin is blackened. Place in bowl and cover with plastic wrap for 15 minutes; then peel and roughly chop peppers. Place in bowl of food processor; add remaining ingredients and pulse until combined.

At sunset, as the fishing boats return to Skull Creek, many Islanders are waiting in line for freshly caught blue crab to make these succulent crab cakes.

Cook's Note:
Double this recipe if serving crab cakes as appetizers. They disappear quickly.

DAUFUSKIE SPINDLED OYSTERS
ON BUTTERED OVEN TOAST

We like to serve spindled oysters as appetizers. If you prefer them on a cocktail buffet, omit toast and arrange them on a lettuce-lined serving dish.

Spindled Oysters

1/2 pound thick-cut, smoke-cured bacon
3 dozen shucked oysters
Salt
Black pepper
1 cup flour
18 (5-inch) skewers
1/4 pound butter
1/4 cup dry sherry
8 slices buttered oven toast

Place bacon between sheets of paper toweling in single layer; microwave 2 to 4 minutes, or as necessary to partially cook bacon without browning. Cut bacon into 1-inch pieces.

Blot oysters dry on paper toweling. Season with salt and pepper; dredge in flour. Allowing 2 oysters per skewer, sandwich one piece of bacon between each 2 oysters on skewers.

In wide skillet, heat butter until foaming. Sauté oysters in butter until golden brown on all sides. Add sherry to contents of skillet; deglaze to make pan sauce. Place 2 skewers on each slice of toast and spoon pan sauce over them.

Buttered Oven Toast

To make buttered oven toast: trim crusts from firm white bread. Brush both sides with melted butter and bake at 325 degrees for 20 minutes, turning once after 10 minutes. Set aside.

Yield: 8 first course servings (with 2 skewers for the kitchen crew!)

INDIVIDUAL OYSTER SOUFFLÉS

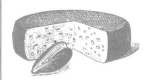

18 fresh shucked oysters
6 cubes of butter, about 1 teaspoon each
2 tablespoons butter
2 tablespoons flour
1/2 teaspoon salt
Dash cayenne
1/4 cup reserved oyster liquid
1 cup milk, heated
3 eggs, separated
1/3 cup grated Parmigiano-Reggiano cheese
1/2 teaspoon cream of tartar
1/4 teaspoon salt

In oyster country, this elegant first course is a lightly textured and delicate variation of more traditional favorites.

Drain oysters but reserve liquid. Place 3 oysters in each of 6 individual soufflé dishes or ramekins, which have been generously buttered. Top each with cube of butter. Set aside.

In saucepan, melt 2 tablespoons butter. Off heat, stir in flour, salt, and cayenne. Whisk in milk and oyster liquid. Return to heat and whisk constantly until thickened. Off heat, whisk in 3 egg yolks which have been well beaten. Whisk in grated cheese. Cool to lukewarm.

Beat 3 egg whites with cream of tartar and salt until firm peaks have formed. Fold into soufflé base. Spoon mixture over oysters, dividing equally among ramekins. Bake at 400 degrees 15 minutes or until puffed and golden. Serve immediately.
Yield: 6 servings

Cook's Note:
To partially prepare in advance: oysters may be placed in soufflé dishes and kept refrigerated. Soufflé base can be made ahead and set aside. A half hour before serving, beat egg whites (see recipe) and fold into base.

CHRISTMAS CAVIAR STARS

When you want to serve
the best, these elegant
hors d'oeuvres are
perfect. Best of all, the
stars can be prepared
4 hours ahead, and filled
just before guests arrive.

1 package (17 1/4-ounce) frozen puff pastry
1 egg beaten with 1 teaspoon water (for glaze)
2/3 cup chilled sour cream
1 (2-ounce) jar black or golden caviar
2 teaspoons chopped fresh chives

Preheat oven to 400 degrees. Thaw one sheet puff pastry, (reserve other sheet for later use) and roll into an 11-inch square, on lightly floured surface. Trim edges neatly, forming 10-inch square. Cut dough into 25 (2-inch) squares. At each corner of one square, cut diagonally toward center (without cutting to center). Fold every other point to center and press to seal. Repeat with remaining squares. Brush lightly with glaze. Transfer to baking sheet. Bake about 12 minutes, or until puffed and golden. Cool on baking sheet.

Spoon sour cream into center of each pastry. Place 1/4 teaspoon caviar on top. Garnish with chives. Yield: 25 servings

ESCARGOTS
IN EDIBLE MUSHROOM SHELLS

1/2 pound butter, softened
5 tablespoons minced fresh parsley, divided
3 cloves garlic, minced
1 1/2 teaspoons lemon juice
1/8 teaspoon salt
1/8 teaspoon freshly ground black pepper
24 uniform mushroom caps, stems removed
24 snails, drained, rinsed, and blotted dry
4 teaspoons grated Parmigiano-Reggiano cheese
8 slices bread, crusts trimmed, and toasted

Incredible edible shells!

A premier first course ...

or when serving

cocktail party style.

Preheat oven to 400 degrees.

Combine butter, half of minced parsley, garlic, lemon juice, salt, and pepper. Spread half of mixture on bottom of shallow pan. Dot each mushroom cap with equal amounts of remaining butter mixture, and place in   prepared pan. Fill each cap with one snail. Sprinkle Parmigiano and remaining parsley over tops of snails.

Bake 10 minutes or until snails are heated through and cheese has melted and turned golden.

For each serving place three mushrooms on slice of toast on individual serving plate. Spoon pan juices evenly over each serving.
Yield: 8 servings

ORANGE SLICES
WITH ANCHOVIES

It's an old tradition among Italian families to nibble on these little appetizers before getting serious about dinner on Christmas Eve.

2 medium navel oranges
1 (2-oz) can flat anchovies, packed in oil, drained
Coarsely ground black pepper
Extra virgin olive oil

Remove ends from unpeeled oranges. Cut into 1/8-inch thick slices and arrange on serving plate. In center of each orange slice, criss-cross two anchovies and give an additional sprinkle of olive oil. Season generously with coarse ground black pepper. Fold in half and enjoy.
Yield: 4 servings

SMOKED SALMON
IN ENDIVE LEAVES

At tastings we found this appetizer to be equally delicious on tiny rounds of pumpernickel or English cucumber ... and not too filling before a festive dinner.

4 ounces smoked salmon, chopped
2 teaspoons chopped fresh dill
1 tablespoon capers
1 1/2 tablespoons lemon juice
2 teaspoons finely chopped chives
1/2 teaspoon horseradish mustard
1/8 teaspoon freshly ground pepper
24 Belgian endive leaves
Sour cream
2 sprigs of fresh dill

Combine smoked salmon, dill, capers, lemon juice, chives, mustard, and pepper.

Mix gently with fork. Taste and adjust seasoning. Spoon 1 1/2 teaspoons of salmon mixture onto each endive leaf. Top with tiny tab of sour cream and garnish with dill sprig.
Yield: 24 servings

BAKED BRIE
WITH CRANBERRY CHUTNEY

1 (10-inch) round French Brie cheese, chilled
1 package frozen puff pastry, thawed
3 cups Cranberry Chutney
Egg wash (1 egg yolk, beaten with 1 tablespoon water)

A round of Brie, warmed and melted, enclosed in golden flaky pastry ... outrageous!

With serrated knife, split Brie into two equal rounds. Sandwich one cup Cranberry Chutney between botton and top layers. Place Brie in a 14-inch round, oven-proof dish (i.e. a large quiche dish).

Smoothly cover top and sides of Brie with puff pastry, molding it to fit, and cut away excess at base. (There will be no pastry underneath the Brie.) Use pastry trimmings to make braided edge around top. With sharp knife, cut leaf-shaped pastries and rounds to resemble berries; attach designs with egg wash. Chill until ready to bake.

Before baking, use remaining egg wash to glaze entire surface of the pastry. Spoon remainder of Cranberry Chutney into baking dish around pastry-covered Brie. Bake in preheated 400 degree oven for 20 to 25 minutes or until golden brown.

Let stand 10 minutes before serving. Serve from baking dish with thinly sliced crusty French baguettes.
Yield: 20 to 30 appetizer servings

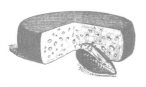

CHEESE & ALMOND PINE CONES

1 1/4 cups blanched whole almonds
1 (8-ounce) package cream cheese, softened
1/2 cup mayonnaise
5 crisply cooked bacon slices, crumbled
1 tablespoon chopped green onion
1/2 teaspoon dried dill (or 1 1/2 teaspoons fresh)
1/8 teaspoon white pepper
Watercress, for garnish

Preheat oven to 300 degrees. Spread almonds in single layer on baking sheet. Bake 15 minutes, stirring often until light brown. Set aside.

Combine cream cheese and mayonnaise. Mix well and add bacon, onion, dill and pepper. Chill overnight to fully develop the flavors.

Next day, divide cheese mixture in two. With dampened hands form each half into shape of pine cone, and arrange on serving plate. Beginning on narrow end, press almonds into cheese at slight angle to resemble pine cones. Continue to overlap until cheese is completely covered. Garnish with crisp, fresh watercress.

Serve with cocktail crackers or sliced French baguette.
Yield: 10 to 12 servings

ASPARAGUS SPEARS
WITH WHITE CHEESE DIPPING SAUCE

A truly scrumptious make-ahead beginning.

1 cup cottage cheese
1/4 cup goat cheese
1/2 cup sour cream
1/4 teaspoon cayenne pepper
1 teaspoon fresh lemon juice
2 tablespoons dry white wine
1/8 teaspoon salt
3 scallions, white part only, minced
3 tablespoons minced fresh chives
3 quarts water
1 tablespoon salt
4 pounds asparagus

In bowl of food processor, place first seven ingredients; process until smooth. Transfer to small bowl and stir in scallions and chives. Cover and chill at least 2 hours.

To large flat non-reactive pan, add 3 quarts water and 1 tablespoon salt; bring to boil.

Meanwhile, break or cut away woody ends of asparagus and peel with vegetable peeler, if desired. In two batches, drop asparagus into boiling water. Boil about 3 or 4 minutes, or until crisp tender. Remove asparagus and quickly plunge into ice water to stop cooking and preserve color.

To serve, place container of cheese sauce in center of large round platter, and surround with asparagus. Yield: 20 to 25 servings

SAVORY PECANS

Spicy holiday pecans

with a pronounced

southern accent.

2 tablespoons olive oil
1 tablespoon rosemary, finely crumbled
1/2 teaspoon cumin
1/4 teaspoon cayenne
1/2 teaspoon thyme
2 garlic cloves, peeled and minced
2 cups pecan halves
Coarsely ground salt to taste

Preheat oven to 350 degrees. In medium skillet, heat oil, add spices and continue to heat. Stir constantly about 3 minutes or just until spices release their aroma. Add pecans and stir to coat well. Spoon into rimmed baking pan large enough to hold nuts in single layer. Bake until nicely browned, shaking pan occasionally, about 12 to 15 minutes.

Remove from oven and sprinkle with coarsely ground salt. Cool and store in airtight container. Can be served warm or cold.
Yield: 2 cups

OLIVE & PECAN CROSTINI

Crostini
Preheat oven to 325 degrees. Slice French baguettes 1/2-inch thick. Place on cookie sheets and brush or spray both sides with olive oil. Bake 20 minutes, turning once after 10 minutes. Best when fresh, but do well in airtight storage containers.

1 (3-ounce) package cream cheese, softened
1 cup sour cream
1 tablespoon minced onion
1 teaspoon minced chives
Dash Tabasco sauce
1/2 cup ripe olives, pitted and coarsely chopped
1/2 cup chopped pecans, toasted
36 unbroken pecan halves, toasted
Crostini

In food processor, mix together cream cheese, sour cream, onion, chives and Tabasco. Transfer mixture to mixing bowl and stir in olives and chopped pecans. Spread evenly on one side of crostini. Place pecan half on top of each. Serve from an attractive serving plate.
Yield: 36 appetizers

BAKED ROSEMARY OLIVES

3 1/2 cups mixed olives
1 cup dry white wine
1/4 cup extra virgin olive oil
2 (4-inch) sprigs rosemary
Zest of 1 orange, and the orange quartered
1/3 cup extra virgin olive oil
2 tablespoons snipped rosemary
2 tablespoons chopped parsley
1 tablespoon minced garlic
1/4 teaspoon freshly ground pepper

This new way with olives from creative Napa Valley chefs has found it's way to more than one Island party table.

Preheat oven to 375 degrees. In a 10 x 15-inch rimmed baking sheet, combine olives, wine, oil, sprig of rosemary, and zest and quartered orange (squeeze orange to release juices). Bake, stirring occasionally, for 45 minutes or until most of liquid has been absorbed.

Return olives to medium-sized container; discard rosemary sprigs and orange quarters; stir in remaining ingredients. Cover and refrigerate. Keeps well.
Yield: 3 1/2 cups

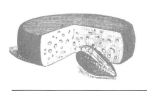

CHRISTMASY HUSH PUPPIES

While hush puppies were created in the south to accompany fish frys, they got their name from cooks who threw scraps to barking dogs while calling out, "hush puppies!" On Hilton Head, with the addition of spices, scallions, and pimiento, they are served as festive cocktail party fare.

1 cup white cornmeal
1/2 cup all-purpose flour
1 teaspoon sugar
1/4 teaspoon garlic powder
1/4 teaspoon black pepper
1/8 teaspoon cayenne pepper
1 egg, beaten
1/3 cup minced green scallions (including green tops)
1 tablespoon chopped pimiento
2/3 cup buttermilk (approximately)
Vegetable oil for frying

Combine dry ingredients in large bowl. Mix well. Add egg, scallions, pimiento and enough buttermilk to make thick batter. While batter is standing, heat oil in deep frying pan, 1/2 inch deep.

Drop batter by rounded teaspoonsful into hot oil, turning once, for 3 to 4 minutes, or until golden and floating. Drain on paper towels. Serve piping hot. Yield: 20

RED POTATO & DILL FOCACCIA

2 (1/4-ounce) envelopes active dry yeast
1 teaspoon granulated sugar
1 cup warm water (110 degrees)
1/2 cup extra virgin olive oil
2 teaspoons kosher salt
2 1/4 cups all-purpose flour
2 medium red potatoes, boiled with skin on
1 1/2 tablespoons chopped fresh dill

Just when you think you've tasted the best focaccia ever, a challenger comes along.

Dissolve yeast with sugar in the warm water and "proof" for about 10 minutes, or until yeast has bubbled up.

In large mixing bowl, combine 6 tablespoons olive oil, salt, flour, and yeast. Mix with wooden spoon, or hands, until dough is smooth. In another large bowl use 1 tablespoon olive oil to coat inside. Transfer dough to oiled bowl, turning until all sides are covered with oil. Cover with plastic wrap until dough has doubled in volume, about 1 hour.

Brush a 12 x 16-inch rimmed baking sheet with olive oil. Punch down dough, transfer to baking sheet and spread, by hand, until pan is filled.

Cover lightly with kitchen towel; let rise about 45 minutes. Meanwhile preheat oven to 400 degrees.

Cut boiled potatoes into 1/4-inch slices. Uncover focaccia dough and press surface with fingers to produce a "dimpled" effect. Cover focaccia with rows of sliced potatoes; sprinkle with fresh dill. Bake 20 to 25 minutes. Cut into squares to serve.
Yield: 40 squares

OLDE ENGLISH SPICED BEEF

Boldly flavored spiced beef is a great favorite among the guys, especially when served with good country bread, horseradish, and mustard with a bite.

1 (8-pound) bottom round of beef, well trimmed with all fat removed
1 ounce salt petre (available in pharmacies)
3/4 cup pickling salt
2 tablespoons brown sugar
2 tablespoons black pepper
2 tablespoons ground allspice
2 teaspoons ground cloves
1 teaspoon mace
2 tablespoons finely crushed bay leaves

Mix together salt petre, salt and brown sugar. Rub mixture over surface of beef and place in large plastic bag. Seal tightly and refrigerate 48 hours, turning once.

Remove beef from bag and place on large tray. Combine remaining spices and rub into all surfaces. Return beef to bag, place bag in large bowl and refrigerate. Turn daily for 2 to 3 weeks, kneading spices and accumulated liquid into beef without removing from bag.

To cook: place meat and accumulated liquid in Dutch oven. Barely cover with water. Bring to boil, reduce heat and simmer gently for 2 hours. Let cool in liquid in Dutch oven for 24 hours, weighted with a heavy plate. Remove from liquid, drain, wrap well, and refrigerate until needed. To serve, slice very thin. Yield: 30 appetizer servings

TERRINE OF CHICKEN LIVER PATÉ IN ASPIC

1 small onion, minced
1 clove garlic, pressed
1 cup butter, melted
1 pound chicken livers, washed and trimmed
1 tablespoon Marsala
1/2 teaspoon salt
1/2 teaspoon allspice
Dash Tabasco sauce
1/2 cup chopped toasted pecans
2 tablespoons Cognac or brandy
3 unbroken pecan halves, toasted

This appetizer gets high marks for its visual appeal and richness of flavor... easy to make, a delight to serve, and recipe can be easily doubled.

Sauté onion and garlic in melted butter 2 or 3 minutes. Add chicken livers and next 4 ingredients. Simmer together for 10 minutes. Transfer chicken liver mixture to bowl of blender. Blend until well combined. Add Cognac or brandy and stir in chopped pecans. Spoon mixture into terrine. Arrange pecan halves on top. Cool to room temperature and spoon aspic over top, covering pecan garnish, to depth of about 1/8th-inch.

Refrigerate 2 hours. Serve surrounded with thinly sliced French baguette.

The Aspic
1/2 envelope unflavored gelatin
3/4 cup beef consommé
1/4 cup water

Soften gelatin in small amount of consommé diluted with water; add remainder of consommé and stir until dissolved. Heat to just below boiling, remove from heat and cool.
Yield: 8 servings

ANGEL BISCUITS
WITH SMITHFIELD HAM

There is rarely a party on Hilton Head without these dainty country-style biscuits. They are split to hold slivers of salty country ham that are often spread with a good quality artichoke relish citrus marmalade, or curried cranberry chutney.

2 packages active dry yeast
1/4 cup warm water (105 to 115 degrees)
2 cups buttermilk
5 to 5 1/4 cups all-purpose flour
1/4 cup sugar
1 tablespoon baking powder
1 teaspoon baking soda
3/4 teaspoon salt
1 cup solid vegetable shortening
1/4 cup melted unsalted butter
1 pound paper thin Smithfield Ham, for filling biscuits

Combine yeast and warm water in small bowl; let stand 5 minutes. Stir in buttermilk and set aside.

Combine remaining dry ingredients in large bowl; cut in shortening with pastry blender until mixture resembles coarse meal. Add buttermilk mixture, stirring with fork until dry ingredients are just moistened. Turn biscuit dough out onto lightly floured surface, and knead 2 minutes.

Roll dough out to 1/2-inch thickness; cut with a 1 1/2-inch biscuit cutter. Place biscuits on lightly greased baking sheet and brush tops with melted butter. Cover with cloth or towel and let rise in warm place (85 degrees), free from drafts, for 1 hour.

Preheat oven to 400 degrees. Bake for 10 to 15 minutes or until tops are lightly browned.
Yield: about 3 dozen

CHAFING DISH
MINCE-MEATBALLS

2 eggs, well beaten
1/3 cup fine dry bread crumbs
1 (2 1/4-ounce) tin of deviled ham
1/8 teaspoon dry mustard
1/2 teaspoon salt
1 pound ground beef
1 (22-ounce) can mincemeat
1/3 cup apple juice
1 tablespoon cider vinegar

These slightly sweet and spicy meatballs make a remarkable chafing dish appetizer.

Preheat oven to 375 degrees. Combine eggs, bread crumbs, deviled ham, dry mustard and salt. Add ground beef and mix well. Shape into 6 dozen 1/2-inch meatballs. Place meatballs, in single layer, in shallow baking pan. Bake 12 minutes, turn once. Remove, drain, cover, and chill.

When ready to serve combine mincemeat, apple juice, and vinegar in saucepan. Heat until bubbling; add meatballs until heated through. Thin with more apple juice if mixture becomes too thick. Transfer to, and serve from chafing dish.
Yield: servings for 10 to 12

MEATBALLS ELLINGHAUS
WITH CAPER SAUCE

Not ordinary meatballs!

The creamy caper sauce

comes through with

every bite.

To prepare as a

main dish, serve over

wide egg noodles.

1/2 pound ground beef

1/2 pound ground veal

1/2 pound ground pork

2 medium onions, diced

1 1/4 teaspoons salt

1/4 teaspoon black pepper

1 /2 cup butter

1/2 cup all-purpose flour

2 1/4 cups water

1 tablespoon corn starch

1/4 cup capers

1 tablespoon caper juice from bottle

Combine beef, veal, pork, onions, salt and pepper in a bowl. Knead mixture well and form into 1-inch meatballs. Set aside.

Melt butter in large pot; add flour and cook until light brown in color. Add water, cornstarch, capers and caper juice. Stir while cooking to creamy consistency. Add meatballs and simmer gently for approximately 45 minutes, stirring frequently. Yield: 12 servings

SWEET & SOUR
KIELBASA

2 (12-ounce) Kielbasa sausages, sliced 1/4-inch thick
1 (12-ounce) bottle prepared chili sauce
3/4 cup red currant jelly
2 teaspoons prepared mustard
1 teaspoon lemon juice
1 (20-ounce) can pineapple chunks, drained

In large skillet cook Kielbasa over low heat for 8 to 10 minutes. Drain off excess fat and set aside. To same skillet stir in chili sauce, jelly, mustard and lemon juice. Add pineapple and Kielbasa. Simmer combination for about 15 minutes. Transfer to chafing dish for serving.
Yield: 24 servings

If you can't find your partner at the party ... check the crowd at the buffet table devouring this Polish-American favorite.

THE ADAMS FAMILY
CHRISTMAS TREE

1 pound liverwurst
1 (8-ounce) package cream cheese, softened
2 tablespoons Worcestershire sauce
Dash Tabasco sauce
1 teaspoon garlic salt
1/2 cup mayonnaise
1/2 cup chopped parsley
6 pimento-stuffed olives, sliced

Combine first six ingredients in bowl of food processor. Blend thoroughly. Spoon mixture onto serving plate; with metal spatula flatten evenly until 1/2-inch thick. Continue shaping to resemble a Christmas tree. Pat minced parsley evenly on sides of tree. Place sliced olives on ends of tree branches to resemble red and green ornaments. Serve with cocktail crackers.
Yield: 15 to 20 appetizer servings

"We've been making this liverwurst Christmas tree for 25 years. Sometimes, at Thanksgiving, we make it shaped like a turkey, and on Super Bowl Sunday it becomes a football. It's imaginative, fun, and fast to disappear!"

THE LOWCOUNTRY OYSTER ROAST

Once you leave Interstate 95 and start to hug the shores of South Carolina, and meander through saltwater marshes, your mouth waters for tastes of the Lowcountry. As you cross the bridge over the Intracoastal waterway you can hardly wait to start peeling shrimp, cracking crabs, and shucking oysters.

The Lowcountry Oyster Roasts are our southern picnic, and a big part of our Yuletide celebrations. It's a customary New Year's Day party in these parts.

Every fall when the 'R' months are back, (you don't eat local oysters in a month without an 'R' in it, as they are protected by law during spawning season), friends get together, buy a couple of bushels of oysters down on the docks, and the party is on.

Dedicated oyster lovers clear a large circle near a water source, dig down about six inches, and lay a fire of oak logs and charcoal. A sturdy sheet metal platform, often held up by bricks, is placed over the fire pit. About an hour before the roast, the fire is lighted, the oysters hosed down to wash off any mud, and opened ones are thrown away.

When the fire is hot, oysters are spread in a single layer in the middle, covered with burlap bags and saturated with lots of water to build up steam. When shells first crack open, the oysters are scooped up with a shovel and dumped on picnic tables.

Opening an oyster is strictly a matter of leverage. Using a strong pointed oyster knife with a guard, the rounded end of the oyster is held with a cloth or towel and pressed firmly against the work surface. The hinged, pointed end is located and the knife is pushed between the shells and twisted to loosen ... until a click is heard. Then, scraping close to the top shell the muscle is cut and the released oyster is ready to be served with a spicy cocktail sauce.

COMFORT SOUPS & SALAD JOYS

Some of the best examples

of international flavors

are found in 'Soups and Salads',

which make them a natural for

Hilton Head entertaining.

Steaming soups are the comfort of this

glorious season,

while colorful salads add the sparkle

to a perfect holiday meal.

CAROLINA SHE-CRAB SOUP

2 tablespoons butter
2 tablespoons finely minced onion
1 tablespoon all-purpose flour
2 cups low- fat milk
2 cups half and half
1/2 teaspoon Worcestershire sauce
Bay leaf
Pinch mace
1/2 teaspoon salt
1/4 teaspoon freshly ground pepper
1/2 teaspoon tomato paste
1 teaspoon finely grated lemon rind
2 cups crab meat, carefully picked over for bits of shell
and cartilage
3 tablespoons crab roe, if available, or
1 tablespoon finely sieved hard-cooked egg yolk
Sherry for soup bowls
Cayenne to sprinkle on each serving

This may be He-Crab Soup if you can't find the roe! Either way, Islanders like to think of it as the signature dish of the Lowcountry.

In the top of a double boiler, over medium heat, melt butter. Add minced onion and sauté gently until just softened. Stir in flour and cook gently for a few minutes without browning. Place pan over simmering water; add milk, half and half, Worcestershire sauce, bay leaf, mace, salt, pepper, tomato paste and grated lemon rind. Cook, stirring frequently, for 15 minutes.

Add crab meat and roe, if available, and cook for 10 minutes longer. Remove from heat, take out bay leaf, and adjust seasoning if necessary.

Place 1 1/2 to 2 teaspoons sherry in each of 6 heated bowls. Divide soup among bowls and garnish with a sprinkling of cayenne.
Yield: 6 servings

OYSTER CORN CHOWDER

In the Lowcountry, adding corn to seafood stews, soups, and chowders is more than just another flavor...

it's a ritual.

4 tablespoons butter
1 large onion, chopped
2 celery stalks, chopped
2 potatoes, peeled and diced into 1/2-inch cubes
2 carrots, peeled and diced into 1/4-inch cubes
1/4 cup chopped Italian parsley
3 cups half and half
1 (7-ounce) can cream-style corn
1/2 teaspoon sugar
1/4 teaspoon freshly ground pepper
1 teaspoon salt, or adjust to taste
1 pint oysters with juice
Chopped parsley for garnish

Melt butter in large soup pot. Add onion and celery and sauté, stirring occasionally, until soft. Add potatoes, carrots, parsley and 2 cups half and half. Simmer, uncovered, 15 minutes or until potatoes are tender. Stir in corn, remaining half and half, sugar, pepper, and salt.

The chowder may be refrigerated, overnight, at this point. Before serving, add oysters with their juice. Simmer 4 to 5 minutes or until edges of oysters curl. Garnish with chopped parsley. Serve immediately with oyster crackers.
Yield: 8 servings

PLANTATION STYLE
SEAFOOD GUMBO

*The lusty soup of
Lowcountry fishermen
features not only seafood
from our waters but okra
from our fields.*

3 tablespoons olive oil
1 medium onion, peeled and diced
1 cup chopped green onion
2 ribs celery, diced
1 cup chopped green bell pepper
1 cup sliced okra (fresh or frozen)
1 (16-ounce) can diced tomatoes
2 cups clam juice
2 cups water
Sprig of thyme
2 or 3 bay leaves
1/4 cup brown roux (see cook's note below)
1 1/2 pounds raw shrimp, peeled and deveined
1 pint raw oysters with liquid
1 filet of white fish, cubed
Salt and pepper to taste
Dash Tabasco sauce

Heat olive oil in soup kettle. Add the two onions, celery, and bell pepper. Sauté until beginning to brown. Add okra and tomato. Cook until heated through. Add tomato juice, clam juice, water, thyme and bay leaves. Stir in brown roux. Bring to a boil. Simmer covered about 1 hour. Taste and correct seasoning by addition of salt, pepper, and Tabasco as desired.

Add shrimp and oysters, cover and simmer 10 minutes. Ladle into soup bowls over scoops of rice.

Cook's Note: To make Brown Roux: combine 3 tablespoons each butter and flour. Cook over moderate heat until nut brown (but not burned). Stir in 1 teaspoon Filé before adding to gumbo mixture.
Yield: 8 servings

TURKEY BONE SOUP

Never throw away the turkey carcass until you have captured every ounce of flavor. This warming soup both charms and nourishes those who drop in after the holidays.

3 quarts stock made from turkey bones (see Cook's Note)
1 cup chopped onion
1/2 cup barley
3 carrots, sliced into 1/2-inch rounds
3 cups cut-up left-over turkey
12 cremini mushrooms, quartered and previously sautéed
1 (12-ounce) package baby frozen peas
1 teaspoon salt, or to taste
1/4 teaspoon freshly ground pepper
Chopped fresh parsley for garnish or
1/2 cup freshly grated Parmigiano-Reggiano cheese

In large soup kettle, bring turkey stock to a boil. Add onions and barley. Reduce heat and cook covered about 40 minutes or until barley is almost tender. Add carrots, turkey, and mushrooms. Continue to simmer about 20 minutes. Add salt and pepper to taste. Add green peas, turn off heat and cover until serving time. Garnish individual servings with minced parsley or grated cheese, or both.

Cook's Note: To make turkey bone stock, break up turkey carcass and place in soup pot. Cover with cold water and add: 2 cups chopped celery, 4 chopped carrots, 4 quartered onions, 2 cloves garlic, 12 peppercorns, 1 bay leaf, 1 teaspoon salt and a handful of fresh parsley. Bring to boil, skim, partially cover and lower heat. Simmer 3 to 4 hours. Strain and refrigerate. Remove solidified fat from surface before using.

Yield: 10 servings

BISQUE OF WILD RICE

1/4 cup butter
2 large onions, peeled and chopped
4 cups celery with leaves, chopped
2 cups diced carrots
1 pound white mushrooms, sliced
1/2 cup butter
1/2 cup all-purpose flour
2 teaspoons salt
1 teaspoon freshly ground pepper
6 cups low-fat milk
2 cups low-salt chicken stock
3 1/2 cups cooked wild rice (cooked by package directions)

Like chicken soup, this is great comfort food. It can easily be made ahead and refrigerated or frozen.

In large non-reactive skillet over medium high heat, place butter and heat till melted and foamy. Add onions, carrots and celery. Sauté until soft but not brown, about 5 minutes. Add mushrooms and continue to sauté until all vegetables are tender. Remove from heat and set aside.

Melt 1/2 cup butter in large Dutch oven or soup pot. Add flour, salt and pepper; stirring constantly until smooth and cook 1 minute. Reduce heat to medium. Gradually add 6 cups low-fat milk and 2 cups chicken stock; cook, stirring constantly until mixture is thickened and bubbly. Stir in sautéed vegetables and wild rice. Adjust seasoning. Reduce heat to low and simmer 15 minutes. Serve in heated bowls.

Yield: 12 (8-ounce) servings

MARVELOUS MUSHROOM SOUP

The refined lightness of this full-flavored mushroom soup makes a fine starter for any elegant meal.

2 tablespoons butter

3 minced shallots

1 1/2 pounds cremini mushrooms, finely chopped

6 cups low-salt chicken broth

1/2 teaspoon salt or to taste

Freshly ground white pepper

1 teaspoon lemon juice

1 lemon, thinly sliced

2 tablespoons finely chopped parsley

In large non-reactive saucepan over medium heat, melt butter; add shallots and cook until soft and transparent. Add mushrooms and cook 5 minutes longer, stirring occasionally. Add chicken broth and simmer uncovered for 30 minutes. Strain through coarse sieve, pressing mushroom bits through. Add salt, pepper, and lemon juice; adjust seasoning if necessary.

Serve in heated bowls, garnished with lemon slices and chopped parsley.
Yield: 4 servings

GULLAH
YAM & PEANUT SOUP

1/4 cup unsalted butter

1/2 cup chopped yellow onion

1/2 cup chopped celery

6 cups peeled and sliced yams (about 2 pounds)

2 quarts poultry stock or low-salt chicken broth

1 1/4 cups smooth peanut butter

Salt and freshly ground black pepper to taste

Chopped roasted peanuts for garnish

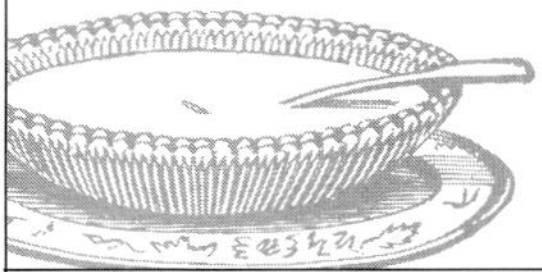

You can't get any more Southern than peanuts and yams!
Serve in individual bowls garnished with chopped roasted peanuts.

In soup pot, melt butter over medium heat. Add onion, celery, and yams. Sauté until onion and celery are soft, but not browned, about 5 minutes. Add stock or broth and bring to boil. Reduce heat to low; cover and simmer until yams are very tender, about 30 minutes. Remove from heat and cool slightly. Working in batches, transfer soup to food processor or blender. Add peanut butter and purée until smooth. Season to taste with salt and pepper. Transfer to clean saucepan and heat over low heat; do not boil.

Yield: 6 to 8 servings

BUTTERNUT HARVEST SOUP

As the days grow shorter,

what an ideal way to

start longer evenings.

6 cups chicken stock or low-salt chicken broth

3 cups peeled, seeded, and chopped butternut squash

2 cups sliced, peeled, and chopped rutabaga

1 cup peeled and chopped Vidalia onion

1 cup peeled and chopped potato

1 Granny Smith apple, peeled and chopped

1 tablespoon minced garlic

2 teaspoons minced fresh ginger

1/2 cup skim milk

1/4 cup fresh orange juice

1 teaspoon salt

1/2 teaspoon ground white pepper

2 tablespoons orange zest

Combine chicken stock, squash, rutabaga, onion, potato, apple, garlic and ginger in large non-reactive saucepan. Bring to boil, cover, reduce heat, and simmer 35 to 40 minutes or until vegetables are soft.

Purée mixture in food processor and return to cooking pot. Add milk, orange juice, salt and pepper. Whisk thoroughly until smooth. Taste and adjust seasoning if necessary. Can be made ahead and refrigerated or frozen.

Reheat to serve. Serve in heated bowls; garnish with orange zest.

Yield: 8 servings

GINGERALE CHRISTMAS WREATH
WITH CUSTARD CREAM

1 (3-ounce) package lime gelatin
1 (3-ounce) package lemon gelatin
2 cups boiling water
2 cups gingerale, room temperature (open just before using)
1 (20-ounce) can pineapple chunks, drained (reserve juice for topping)
1 cup whole maraschino cherries
1 cup whole seedless green grapes
1/2 cup pecan halves

Combine flavored gelatins in large bowl and stir in 2 cups boiling water, stirring until gelatin is dissolved. Cool and add 2 cups gingerale. Chill until partially set. Add remaining ingredients and spoon into large ring mold. Chill until firmly set. Unmold onto large serving plate and fill center with custard cream.

Custard Cream
1/2 cup granulated sugar
1/4 cup reserved pineapple juice
2 tablespoons fresh lemon juice
2 eggs, beaten
1/8 teaspoon salt
1 cup whipping cream, whipped until soft peaks form

Combine sugar, juices, eggs and salt in heavy saucepan and cook over medium heat until thickened, stirring constantly. Remove from heat and cool. Gently fold in whipped cream.
Yield: 8 servings

An edible Christmas wreath that literally shimmers at the holiday table.

HERITAGE PINEAPPLE LIME MOLD

"Because this salad is so pretty and refreshing, it has been part of our family celebrations for as long as we can remember."

1 (3-ounce) package cream cheese, softened
1 (3-ounce) package lime gelatin
1 (8-ounce) can crushed pineapple, undrained
1/2 cup chopped walnuts or pecans
12 quartered maraschino cherries
1 (5-ounce) jar small pimiento-stuffed olives, drained
1 cup whipping cream
Italian parsley for garnish

Place cream cheese in medium sized bowl. Add lime gelatin and blend thoroughly. Bring pineapple to boil in small pan and pour over cheese mixture. Chill for 1 hour or until mixture begins to set.

Fold in nuts, cherries and olives. Whip cream until soft peaks form and gently fold into fruit and cheese mixture. Spoon into decorative 1-quart mold and chill several hours or overnight. Unmold onto serving plate and garnish with Italian parsley sprigs.

Yield: 6 servings

APPLAUSE APPLE SALAD

"This healthy and colorful winter salad pleases all audiences, especially when costumed with cranberries and oranges for seasonal productions."

1 3/4 cups peeled, cored, and grated tart apples (Granny Smith)
1 cup peeled and grated carrots
3 to 4 tablespoons olive oil and vinegar dressing
3 to 4 tablespoons whole cranberry sauce
Mint sprigs and orange slices

In medium bowl, combine grated apples and carrots. Add enough dressing to moisten. For a festive touch, add 4 tablespoons whole cranberry sauce and mix in well.

Serve at room temperature garnished with mint sprigs and orange slices, or chill until serving time.

Yield: 6 servings

RUBY
CRAN-RASPBERRY RING

1 (3-ounce) package raspberry gelatin
1 cup boiling water
1 (16-ounce) can whole cranberry sauce
1 (10-ounce) package frozen raspberries, thawed and drained

Add boiling water to raspberry gelatin and stir until dissolved. Mix in cranberry sauce and drained raspberries. Pour into a 1-quart ring mold and chill. At serving time, unmold onto an attractive serving dish. Garnish as desired.
Yield: 6 servings

To unmold a gelatin salad, loosen gelatin by carefully running the tip of a knife around rim of mold. Invert mold onto a serving plate. Apply a hot moist towel to outer surface of mold for one minute and remove. Gently shake mold to release gelatin.

GEBHARDT'S
RHINELANDER KOHL SLAW

1 medium, firm head of green cabbage
1 to 2 tablespoons salad oil
1 to 3 tablespoons apple cider vinegar
1 large carrot, grated
1 tablespoon mayonnaise
1 to 2 tablespoons heavy cream
Salt and pepper to taste
Granulated sugar to taste
1/2 teaspoon celery seed

Cut cabbage into quarters and finely shred as thin as possible. Toss cabbage with salad oil to coat evenly and drizzle with vinegar. Add grated carrot, mayonnaise, heavy cream and celery seed. Season to taste with salt and pepper. Add enough granulated sugar to offset tartness of vinegar. Make at least 4 hours ahead for flavors to develop and blend. Before serving, taste once more, and adjust seasoning.
Yield: 6 to 8 servings

Usually thought of as picnic food, this cole slaw is particularly refreshing on a party table featuring cold sliced meats and cheeses.

GINGERED PEARS
& LINGONBERRIES

"A lovely pear salad of Swedish origin, reminiscent of holidays in Minnesota."

1 cup granulated sugar

1/2 cup white wine

1 cup water

2-inch piece fresh ginger, peeled and sliced

1 stick cinnamon

1 lime or 1/2 lemon, sliced

1 (8-ounce) jar sweetened lingonberries

4 firm ripe Bartlett pears

8 leaves Boston lettuce

In 9-inch skillet combine sugar, wine, water, ginger, cinnamon and lime.

Bring to boil; reduce heat to simmer. Meanwhile, peel pears, split in half lengthwise and remove cores. Place in poaching liquid cut-side down. Cover and simmer until tender. Poaching time will vary depending upon ripeness.

When pears are tender, cool in poaching liquid. Store in refrigerator until needed. To serve, drain and fill cavities with lingonberries. Arrange on lettuce lined salad plates.

Yield: 8 servings

WATERCRESS, APPLE & ROQUEFORT ON GREENS

2 tablespoons minced shallots
2 tablespoons champagne or rice vinegar
2 tablespoons fresh lemon juice
1/2 teaspoon freshly ground pepper
1/2 teaspoon salt
2/3 cup walnut oil (or combination of walnut and olive oil)
2 bunches watercress, washed, and leaves separated from stems
1 small head Romaine, washed and cut into fine julienne
1 head Boston lettuce, washed and torn
2 Red Delicious apples, cored and thinly sliced
2/3 cup walnut pieces, toasted
2/3 cup crumbled Roquefort cheese

A special occasion salad anytime of the year ... especially at Yuletide!

In small bowl, combine shallots, vinegar, lemon juice, pepper and salt. Gradually whisk in oil to make vinaigrette.

In chilled salad bowl, combine watercress, Romaine, and Boston lettuce. Add apples and nuts; toss with enough dressing to just coat leaves. Divide salad among 6 chilled salad plates and top with Roquefort cheese.

Cook's Note: 1) In warmer climates, Roquefort is easier to crumble if first placed in freezer about 15 minutes. 2) To maintain color of apples, slice them at last minute or toss with small amount of lemon juice. Yield: 6 servings

ASIAN MANGO & CHICKEN ON NAPA

During recipe testing, this salad became a favorite. Made with chicken it is a light entrée, without chicken it makes an interesting starter for a holiday meal.

6 chicken breast halves, boned and skinned
2 tablespoons peanut oil
1/2 cup prepared Baste and Glaze Teriyaki Sauce
1 head Napa cabbage
1 yellow bell pepper, seeded and slivered lengthwise
1 orange bell pepper, seeded and slivered lengthwise
2 ripe mangos, pitted, peeled and sliced length-wise
Soy-Ginger Vinaigrette (recipe follows)

With heavy knife, flatten chicken breasts between sheets of wax paper to same thickness.

Heat peanut oil in skillet. Sauté chicken breasts about 3 minutes on each side. Pour teriyaki sauce over chicken breasts in skillet; increase heat, and turn chicken repeatedly until glazed on both sides. Remove to side dish and cool. Cut into 1/2-inch strips.

Meanwhile, finely shred Napa cabbage to equal 6 cups. Place cabbage on large oval serving platter. Arrange bell peppers and mango slices on cabbage. Layer chicken strips on top. Using plastic dispenser bottle, drizzle entire salad with Soy-Ginger Vinaigrette.

Soy-Ginger Vinaigrette
1/2 cup seasoned rice vinegar
1 teaspoon dark sesame oil
1 tablespoon soy sauce
1 teaspoon grated fresh ginger root
1/4 cup peanut or vegetable oil

Place all ingredients in plastic dispenser bottle. Shake to combine.

Yield: 6 salad servings

SWEDISH HERRING SALAD
(SILLSALLED)

1 cup cooked, cubed potatoes
1 cup cooked, cubed carrots
1 cup cubed Granny Smith apples
1/2 cup minced onion
1 Kosher dill pickle, finely cubed
3 cups cubed pickled beets
2 cups plain salt herring, cut into small pieces
1/4 teaspoon white pepper
1/2 cup extra virgin olive oil

Lettuce for service plate
2 hard-cooked eggs, peeled and chopped
4 tablespoons chopped fresh dill
Extra dill sprigs
1 1/2 cups dairy sour cream
Thinly sliced dark bread

Mix first eight ingredients gently, adding olive oil gradually as you turn the ingredients. When all ingredients are evenly combined, pack mixture into oiled ring mold, or other decorative mold, as desired. Cover and chill several hours. For best flavor, make on day of party.

To serve: unmold onto lettuce lined serving dish. Garnish top with chopped hard-cooked eggs and minced dill. Arrange dill sprigs around salad. Serve with sour cream and thinly sliced dark bread.
Yield: 12 servings

Sillsalled is a wonderful salad to have on a festive food table or as a hearty hors d'oeuvre ... color is spectacular!

JINGLE BELL CRANBERRIES ON BOSTON LETTUCE

A salad that uses tender greens to balance the flavors of candied fruit and sweet-sour dressing.

2 cups fresh cranberries, washed and picked over
1 cup granulated sugar
2 heads Boston lettuce
1 (11-ounce) can mandarin oranges, drained
2 tablespoons honey
2 tablespoons cider vinegar
1 teaspoon dry mustard
Dash salt
1 teaspoon poppy seeds
3 tablespoons orange juice
3/4 cup vegetable oil
Salt and freshly ground black pepper, to taste

Preheat oven to 350 degrees. Spread cranberries in a shallow baking dish and distribute sugar evenly over them. Cover dish tightly with foil and bake 1 hour, stirring occasionally. Cool to room temperature and refrigerate until needed or up to 2 days.

To make dressing: in a small bowl, whisk honey, vinegar, mustard, salt, poppy seeds and orange juice. Slowly whisk in oil until well blended. Use immediately, or refrigerate until needed, up to 2 days.

To serve: toss lettuce and oranges with dressing to coat greens lightly. Season to taste with salt and pepper. Divide among chilled salad plates and garnish top generously with candied cranberries.

Yield: 8 servings

CHRISTMAS SPINACH SALAD

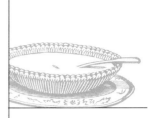

1 pound fresh spinach, washed, dried and stemmed
1 pint fresh strawberries, washed, hulled, and halved
1/4 cup granulated sugar
2 tablespoons sesame seeds
1 tablespoon poppy seeds
1 1/2 teaspoons minced onion
1/4 teaspoon Worcestershire sauce
1/4 teaspoon paprika
1/2 cup canola and olive oil mix
1/4 cup cider vinegar

Tear spinach into bite-sized pieces. Combine gently with strawberries in large salad bowl. To make salad dressing combine remaining ingredients in bowl of blender. Cover and blend at low speed for 30 seconds. Drizzle dressing over spinach and strawberries. Toss gently and serve immediately.
Yield: 4 servings

This light spinach salad is a perfect complement to the richness of many holiday menus. Try it with turkey sandwiches the day after Thanksgiving!

NEW YEAR'S EVE "CAESAR"

1/4 cup olive oil
1 teaspoon Worcestershire sauce
1/8 teaspoon freshly ground pepper
1/4 teaspoon each, salt and dry mustard
Juice of 1/2 lemon
1 or 2 garlic cloves, finely minced
2 heads Romaine lettuce, washed, dried, and torn
1/4 cup crumbled blue cheese
1 cup croutons
6 anchovy fillets, chopped
1/4 cup freshly grated Parmigiano-Reggiano cheese

Combine olive oil, Worcestershire, pepper, salt, mustard, lemon juice and garlic. Stir together and set aside to allow flavors to blend. Place Romaine in a large salad bowl; pour over dressing and toss well. On top scatter the blue cheese, croutons, anchovies and grated cheese. Toss, toss, toss. Serve immediately.
Yield: 4 to 6 servings

The original "Caesar" recipe was created in the 20's. Irene and Jack Williamson liked this verson so much they listed the ingredients on a paper napkin in New York on a special New Year's Eve.

AVOCADO & TOMATO
HOLIDAY SALAD

Make this a day ahead

to highlight

a colorful buffet.

Avocado Layer
1 envelope unflavored gelatin
1/4 cup cold water
1 cup boiling water
1 teaspoon sugar
2 tablespoons lemon juice
1 cup mashed ripe avocado
1/2 cup sour cream
1/2 cup mayonnaise
1 teaspoon salt
Freshly ground pepper and dash of cayenne

Soften gelatin in cold water, add boiling water to dissolve. Add sugar and 1 tablespoon of lemon juice. Chill until slightly thickened. Immediately after mashing avocado, add other tablespoon of lemon juice, sour cream, mayonnaise, salt, pepper and cayenne. Mix thoroughly with chilled gelatin. Pour into 2-quart mold and chill until set.

Tomato Layer
1 envelope unflavored gelatin
1/4 cup cold water
1 cup boiling water
2 tablespoons sugar
1 (10-ounce) can tomato soup
1 tablespoon lemon juice
1/4 teaspoon salt

Soften gelatin in cold water; dissolve in boiling water. Add sugar, soup, lemon juice and salt. Pour over firm avocado layer. Chill until set. Unmold on bed of greens or watercress, surround with small cherry tomatoes. Slice to serve.

Yield: 8 to 10 servings

LAYERED CHICKEN & TOMATO ASPIC

... a vintage layered salad, light and flavorful, perfect for a holiday luncheon .

Tomato Aspic Layer
4 cups tomato juice
1/3 cup chopped onion
1/4 cup chopped celery leaves
2 tablespoons brown sugar
2 small bay leaves
4 whole cloves
2 envelopes unflavored gelatin
1/4 cup cold water
3 tablespoons fresh lemon juice
1 cup finely diced celery
1 cup mixed olives, for garnish

Combine tomato juice, onion, celery leaves, brown sugar, bay leaves and cloves in non-reactive saucepan. Simmer over low heat 5 minutes. While mixture is simmering, soften gelatin in cold water in large bowl. Strain hot aspic mixture over softened gelatin; stir until dissolved; add lemon juice.

Refrigerate until partially set. Fold in diced celery; spoon into 6-cup decorative mold. Refrigerate at least 4 hours or until set.

Chicken Layer
1 envelope unflavored gelatin
1/4 cup cold water
1 cup mayonnaise
1/2 cup water
3 tablespoons fresh lemon juice
2 cups diced cooked chicken
1/2 cup diced celery
2 tablespoons chopped parsley

Soften gelatin in cold water; stir over hot water until dissolved. Blend in mayonnaise, 1/2 cup water and lemon juice. Mix in chicken, celery and parsley. Spoon over aspic layer and chill until set.

To serve: Unmold onto a festive holiday plate, and garnish with olives.
Yield: 8 servings

ANNUAL CULINARY FESTIVALS

As March arrives, Hilton Head erupts in bloom with a magnificent array of azaleas. The air is scented with the early sweetness of Spring. It is the month in which the Culinary Festival season begins.

SpringFest started as a local festival in 1983, and now has become a month long event, recognized world-wide. There is something for everyone – with activities ranging from food competitions and quilt shows to home tours, health fairs, and parades.

When WineFest weekend arrives, a festive gala is held at the Self Family Arts Center in a tented outdoor area, a black-tie dinner that matches up award winning wines and the culinary fantasies of the Island's most noted chefs. Inside the center there are silent and live wine auctions.

The largest tented outdoor public wine tasting on the East coast occurs at picturesque Shelter Cove Harbor, with more than 500 domestic and international wines available for tastings. Commemorative glasses year after year have become collectibles, although the only thing that ever changes is the logo color.

Kitchen Performances is an annual tour of kitchens in Hilton Head's loveliest homes with gourmet samplings from the chefs of our finest restaurants. For the sweet tooth there are ChocolateFest and Sweet Tastes of SpringFest, where amateur and professionals compete for blue ribbons. WingFest is a crowd pleasing nibbler and the Cookbook Fair is a charitable cookbook swap of new and old treasured favorites.

The Rib Burn-off in May delights the entire island as does the Chili Cookoff in the fall. 'Tastes of the Lowcountry' is festive and many local chefs put their spin on our traditional flavors.

The Soup Challenge in October is one of our most outstanding festivals as ACF chefs vie for winning gold medallions, which are highly prized in the culinary world.

Coming full circle, in January and February the International Winter Carnival hosts a Native Islander Gullah Celebration, a JazzFest, and the week long Festa Italiana with an Italian opera and all things Italian.

page 60

$\mathcal{C}$ENTER STAGE ENTRÉES

The warmth and conviviality

of a festively appointed holiday table

capture the essence of the season...

it's where memories are made and traditions shared.

The entrée is key to selecting a menu

that's simple to carry off,

yet has the élan to fit the occasion.

Among these entrées you will find the

traditional and new, stylish and appealing, simple and comforting

... all are island favorites.

WILD MUSHROOM RAGÙ
WITH TORTELLINI

2 cups heavy cream
1 teaspoon salt, divided
Generous grinding fresh nutmeg
4 tablespoons unsalted butter
1/4 cup minced shallots
2 large cloves garlic, minced
1/2 pound each fresh cremini, shiitake and oyster mushrooms
1 large portobello, cut into 2 inch strips, stem peeled and minced
1 cup freshly grated Parmigiano-Reggiano cheese
1/2 teaspoon freshly ground black pepper
1 pound refrigerated cheese tortellini
Fresh mixed herbs, julienned for garnish

This versatile sauce is also perfect with other pasta shapes or with pan-grilled breasts of chicken, veal scallopini, or chops.

In medium saucepan over moderate heat, combine cream, 1/2 teaspoon salt and nutmeg. Bring to boil, lower heat and cook uncovered about 15 minutes or until cream has reduced by one-fourth and become thickened.

Meanwhile, melt butter in large skillet. Add shallots and garlic, cook covered, stirring occasionally, about 4 minutes. Increase heat and add all mushrooms at once along with 1/2 teaspoon salt. Cover and cook until mushrooms begin to render their juices. Uncover and cook over high heat until all juices have evaporated. Stir in reduced cream, 1/3 cup of the grated cheese, and pepper. Cover and keep warm.

Pair with a Chianti Reserva, or any of its relatives, for authentic enjoyment.
If white is preferred try a smooth Italian Pinot Grigio or a Willakenzie Oregon Pinot Gris.

Cook tortellini in large pot of boiling salted water about 3 minutes or until tender. Drain and return to hot pot. Add mushroom sauce to tortellini and toss well. Serve in warmed pasta bowls. Garnish individual servings with julienne of fresh herbs. Pass additional grated cheese.

Yield: 4 entrée servings or 8 first course servings

PENNE WITH SHRIMP
IN TOMATO & VODKA SAUCE

... *a hurry-up dinner*

after a hectic day of

Christmas shopping.

For a real kick,

try flavored vodka

in the sauce.

1 tablespoon butter
1 (28-ounce) can plum tomatoes
l/4 cup chopped, fresh basil
Salt and pepper to taste
1/2 cup vodka
6 tablespoons whipping cream
1 pound uncooked medium shrimp, peeled and deveined
1 pound penne pasta
Fresh basil sprigs

Melt butter in large heavy skillet over medium heat. Add tomatoes, including juices, and bring to a boil. Crush tomatoes with back of wooden spoon. Reduce heat, add chopped basil and simmer 15 minutes. Season with salt and pepper. Add vodka and cream. Boil 3 minutes. Add shrimp and simmer about 3 minutes, turning occasionally, until cooked through.

Meanwhile, cook pasta in large pot of boiling salted water until tender but firm to the bite. Drain well. Add pasta to sauce in skillet and stir to combine and heat through. Divide pasta among pasta bowls and garnish with sprigs of basil.

Yield: 4 entrée servings

If you have a red
California Sangiovese on
hand, try it with this!
(Or any one of the
classic four Italian "B"s:
Barbera, Bardolino,
Barbaresco or Barolo.)
White wine lovers
will prefer a dry,
crisp Gavi
di Gavi.

SALMON
WITH ORIENTAL
MAHOGANY SAUCE

1 1/2 to 2 pounds salmon filets, (2 filets, 1 inch thick)
1 cup canned whole cranberry sauce
1/4 cup honey
1/4 cup soy sauce
2 cloves garlic, minced
1/4 teaspoon black pepper
Fresh minced parsley to garnish

East meets West with a blaze of taste in this simply prepared, yet fabulous entrée.

Preheat oven to 375 degrees. Remove skin from salmon filets with thin sharp knife. Place filets in lightly greased baking dish. Combine cranberry sauce, honey, soy sauce, garlic and black pepper. Spread sauce over filets covering completely. Reserve some sauce to pass. Bake uncovered 20 to 25 minutes, or until sauce is bubbling and salmon flakes easily when pierced with tines of fork.

To serve, slice into individual portions and garnish with minced parsley. Heat reserved sauce to pass for those who just can't get enough of it.

Yield: 6 to 8 servings

Consider pairing this entrée with Madfish Chardonnay – a delightful non-oak style white from Western Australia, crisp and clean, bursting with fruit flavors of mango, papaya and kiwi.

BRAMS POINT
SHRIMP 'N GRITS

No dish is more typically Lowcountry than Shrimp and Grits. Sweet succulent shrimp come from our back-water creeks and stone-ground whole corn grits come from neighboring mills. This version shows our melting pot influence with the addition of olive oil, Parmesan cheese and sweet bell peppers.

The Grits
2 cups stone-ground grits (not instant)
4 cups milk plus 2 cups water
1/2 cup heavy cream
1 stick butter
1/2 cup Parmesan cheese
3 tablespoons minced chives
Salt and pepper to taste

Place grits in bowl and cover with cold water. Skim pith that floats and drain off water. Transfer to non-reactive pot; add milk and water. Cook on low heat, stirring frequently, for 2 or 3 hours. When grits are cooked and thick, add butter, cream, cheese, chives, and salt and pepper to taste.

The Shrimp
3 tablespoons olive oil
2 pounds medium shrimp, peeled and deveined
2 cloves garlic, minced
1 large onion, cut into strips
2 red bell peppers, roasted and peeled
1 yellow bell pepper, roasted and peeled
1/4 cup sherry
Dash Tabasco sauce
3 tablespoons butter
Salt and pepper to taste

Heat olive oil in frying pan on high heat. Add shrimp, stir fry until all turn pink.

Remove to side dish and reserve. Add garlic and onions to pan, stir fry briefly. Cut peppers into strips; add to onions. Continue to stir fry until all ingredients are sizzling. Add sherry, Tabasco, butter, and salt and pepper to taste. Return shrimp to mixture, heat through, and spoon over grits at once.

Yield: 6 to 8 servings

You may prefer an American Chardonnay with this Southern classic. If you're daring see how a light Zinfandel adds even more life to the marriage of Shrimp 'n Grits.

SEA BASS
EN PAPILLOTE

Parchment paper
1/4 cup butter, melted
2 cups sliced leeks
4 sprigs fresh thyme
4 (6-ounce) sea bass or halibut filets, 1-inch thick
Salt and white pepper, to taste
1/4 cup Dijon mustard thinned with
2 tablespoons dry white wine
1/2 cup sliced shallots
1/2 cup finely chopped cucumber
1/2 cup peeled and diced Roma tomatoes
12 whole small shiitake mushroom caps
4 lemon slices

Lay heart-shaped parchment on counter and brush with butter. On right side lay a bed of sliced leeks and a sprig of thyme. Season both sides of filets with salt and white pepper; place on leeks. Brush filets with mustard-wine mixture. Spoon 2 tablespoons each shallot, cucumber and tomato over filets. Arrange mushroom caps beside filets and place lemon slice on top. Fold left side of parchment over filet until edges match

To complete packet and to seal edges, begin at curved end and make a 1/2 inch fold full length of outer edge. Make a pleat every inch along the fold. Repeat folding and pleating process a second time to make double seal. With fingertips press firmly along fold lines to reinforce. Twist tip tightly at bottom to complete seal. (Packets may be made 4 hours ahead and refrigerated.)

Preheat oven to 450 degrees. Place papillotes on baking sheet. Bake 12 to 15 minutes or until puffed. Serve immediately.
Yield: 4 servings

To make papillote packets, cut parchment paper into four 12 x 16-inch lengths. Fold each in half, and cut to shape of half a heart. When unfolded paper will be heart-shaped.

With such a special dish, go the distance with a well balanced Chassagne Montrachet, bottle aged at least five years.

Frogmore Stew knows no season on Hilton Head. The stew originated on nearby St. Helena Island, once known as Frogmore. In the summer we serve this regional specialty on newspaper-covered picnic tables. For the holidays, it is served from huge earthenware platters.

This is usually served with a local beer but a lively red Corbières from the French Languedoc could add even more spice to your enjoyment.

FROGMORE STEW

6 to 7 quarts water

1 (3-ounce) package seafood boil

2 tablespoons sea salt

3 garlic cloves, peeled

1/2 lemon, thinly sliced

2 pounds smoked sausage, in 2-inch lengths

16 small unpeeled redskin potatoes

12 ears shucked corn, in 3-inch lengths

5 pounds large fresh shrimp in the shell

To water in large stock pot, add seafood boil, salt, garlic and lemon. Bring to boil. Add sausage and boil 5 minutes. Add potatoes and boil 15 minutes or until almost done. Add corn; boil 5 minutes more. Add shrimp. When shrimp turn pink and firm, in about 3 minutes, drain ingredients and place on large heated serving platter.

Yield: 8 servings

Cook's Note: Ingredients can be adjusted to serve any number. Allow about 2 teaspoons seafood boil per quart water. Allow 1/2 pound shrimp, 1/4 pound sausage, 1 1/2 ears corn, and 2 potatoes per person.

SOUTHERN
BRUNSWICK STEW

1 (3 1/2 to 4-pound) broiler-fryer chicken, poached, skinned, deboned and cubed

6 cups poaching liquid from chicken

1/4 pound cooked ham, large dice

2 large onions, chopped

1 large green pepper, seeded and chopped

2 tablespoons minced fresh parsley

1 (15-ounce) can crushed tomatoes

1 (14.75-ounce) can creamed corn

1 (10-ounce) package frozen sliced okra

1/2 cup dark brown sugar

1/4 cup fresh lemon juice

1/4 cup Worcestershire sauce

1 tablespoon garlic powder

1 teaspoon dried thyme, crumbled

1 bay leaf

1 teaspoon salt

1/2 teaspoon black pepper

3/4 cup crushed saltines

3/4 cup crushed Ritz crackers

1 cup rice, cooked by package directions

Minced parsley, for garnish

To the 6 cups reserved broth add cubed chicken, ham and all remaining ingredients except saltines, crackers, rice and parsley. Simmer 1/2 hour; remove bay leaf. Add crushed crackers and stir until stew is thickened. Ladle into large bowls. Top with scoop of freshly cooked rice. Garnish with minced parsley.
Yield: 6 to 8 servings

There are as many Brunswick Stew recipes as there are small towns in the South. It is known as the most famous dish to emerge from the campfires and cabins of pioneer Americans. This is an Islander's adaptation from an early Virginia version.

Now is the time for the Gamay grape ... Beaujolais. Voila!

SAUTÉED BREASTS OF CHICKEN
WITH MUSTARD FRUITS

Age-old mustard fruits
are revived for the
holidays ... serve with
chicken, turkey, or pork
cutlets. Everyone will
enjoy the tangy, sweet
flavors of this
tongue-tingling glaze.

Mustard Fruits
1 cup dry white wine
1 cup water
1/2 cup granulated sugar
4 Bartlett pears, peeled, cored and quartered
16 bite-size pitted prunes
16 dried apricot halves
1/4 cup dried cherries, or other dried fruit as available
4 to 6 tablespoons Dijon mustard

Combine wine, water and sugar in skillet and bring to boil. Add fruits. Simmer until pears are tender; remove fruit with slotted spoon. Increase heat; reduce pan juices to about 1/2 cup and sugars have begun to caramelize. Whisk in 4 tablespoons Dijon mustard. Taste, add one or more tablespoons of mustard if sharper contrast in flavor is desired. Return fruit to sauce, turn gently, set aside and keep warm.

Sautéed Chicken Breasts
8 skinless chicken breast halves
1 lemon cut in half
3/4 cup all-purpose flour on plate
Salt and white pepper
1 tablespoon each olive oil and butter

This combination of
sweet and pungent
flavors calls for a crisp
Fumé Blanc. Château
St. Jean's La Petite Etoile
is classic Sonoma
Valley with its
light citrus
delivery.

Between sheets of wax paper, flatten chicken breasts to uniform thickness. Rub each side with lemon juice; sprinkle lightly with salt and white pepper. Dip each chicken breast in flour shaking off excess. Set aside 10 to 15 minutes or until flour no longer appears white.

Heat olive oil and butter in skillet over medium heat. Sauté chicken breasts 4 minutes on each side or until lightly golden. Transfer to heated serving platter and spoon over Mustard Fruits.

Yield 8 servings

ROCK CORNISH HENS
WITH CUMBERLAND SAUCE

4 (1 1/2-pound) Cornish hens
2 tablespoons melted butter
Salt and white pepper
Cumberland Sauce (recipe below)

Prepare Cumberland Sauce; set aside. Preheat oven to 425 degrees. Place rack in shallow roasting pan, and pour about 1/4-inch water in pan. Wash hens and blot dry. Split in half and remove wing tips. With tip of sharp knife, nick the ligament between drumstick and thigh and at joint of wing. Brush all sides with melted butter. Season lightly with salt and white pepper.

Place hens, skin-side-down, leaving space between, on rack in roasting pan. Transfer to oven; reduce heat to 375 degrees. Roast 45 minutes, turning once or twice. Brush with Cumberland Sauce during last 15 minutes and finish roasting skin-side-up. Baste once more during last 5 minutes. Transfer hens to warmed serving platter. Serve with Cumberland Sauce on the side.

A simple recipe such as this can be just the ticket for a light supper for eight. If appetites are running high, invite only 4 or 6. Especially good served with a savory rice pilaf.

Cumberland Sauce
1/2 cup orange juice
1/2 cup red currant jelly
1 tablespoon Dijon mustard
1 tablespoon brown sugar
1 tablespoon lemon juice
1/2 cup red port wine

Combine all ingredients in small sauce pan. Heat to simmer while stirring constantly. Simmer about 5 minutes, set aside and keep warm.
Yield: 8 servings

Simple yet sophisticated – the perfect match is a red Beringer Alluvium, mainly Merlot but in a class by itself with added Cabernet Sauvignon, Cabernet Franc and Petite Verdot. A fine California claret.

QUAIL BRAISED
IN WHITE WINE
WITH TARRAGON CREAM

*Quail are native
American partridges
known in South
Carolina as Bobwhites
for the sound of their
call. The Lowcountry
hunting season falls
during Yuletide and
these delicate
white-fleshed game birds
are celebratory fare.*

16 quail
Salt and paprika
2 tablespoons each butter and oil
1/2 cup dry white wine
1/2 cup chicken broth
1 teaspoon tarragon, crumbled
1/2 teaspoon white pepper
Instant-blend flour, sufficient to thicken sauce
1/2 cup whipping cream
2 tablespoons finely minced parsley

Wash quail and remove any shot you may find. Blot
dry with paper toweling. Truss birds with string.
Season each bird with light sprinkling of salt and
paprika. Heat equal parts of butter and oil in large
chicken fryer or covered fry pan. Brown the birds, a
few at a time, on all sides; remove to side dish when
browned. To skillet add wine, chicken broth, tarragon
and white pepper. As it simmers scrape up any residue
that may have stuck to skillet. Return birds to skillet,
cover and simmer over low heat 25 to 30 minutes.

Remove birds to serving dish, remove string, and keep
warm. Whisk flour into contents of skillet. When
smooth whisk in cream. Cook over high heat until
mixture thickens to desired consistency. Taste and
adjust seasoning.

Spoon sauce over quail and garnish with minced
parsley.
Yield: 8 servings

*Memories of the hunt
could be enhanced with
a Pinot Grigio or
perhaps a crisp
Riesling.*

HOLIDAY DUCK
WITH MANGO SAUCE

1 (4 1/2-pound) Long Island duckling
Salt
1 small lime, quartered
1 bay leaf
2 tablespoons butter
1/2 cup minced red bell pepper
2 1/2 cups cubed fresh mango
1 cup chicken stock
1 1/2 teaspoons grated ginger root
3 tablespoons dry Marsala
1/4 teaspoon salt, and white pepper to taste
1/4 cup minced scallions
2 tablespoons minced fresh parsley

... international flavors from the Island's growing international community.

Preheat oven to 450 degrees. Wash and pat dry cavity of duck. Sprinkle cavity with salt; insert lime and bay leaf. With paper toweling dry skin of duck and prick all over with a skewer. Put duck on rack in roasting pan and sprinkle lightly with salt. Transfer to oven. After 5 minutes reduce heat to 350 degrees. Roast 1 hour and 30 minutes, or until juices run clear when thigh is pricked with skewer.

In saucepan melt butter and cook red pepper about 5 minutes, or until softened. Add half of the mango, chicken stock and ginger; simmer about 15 minutes. Add remaining mango, Marsala, salt and white pepper to taste. Bring mixture to boil and remove from heat. Keep warm.

Such a romantic dish for two deserves the refinement of a good French Burgundy or Pinot Noir from Oregon (both on the same latitude).

Cut duck into serving pieces and arrange on heated platter. Glaze surface with a little of the sauce and transfer remainder to sauce boat. Garnish duck with minced scallion and parsley. (Recipe can easily be doubled or tripled.)
Yield: 2 servings

page 73

ROAST TURKEY BREAST
WITH CARAMELIZED CHESTNUTS

A good choice for the

small family

get-together…

savory and succulent.

The caramelizing seals

in moisture and

enhances flavor.

1 (2-pound) half turkey breast with bone
2 to 3 tablespoons peanut oil
Salt and pepper, to taste
1 cup sugar
2 tablespoons butter
1 cup hot water
1 (16-ounce) jar prepared whole chestnuts
1 pound peeled baby carrots
16 or more plump cloves garlic, peeled

Preheat oven to 450 degrees. Place turkey, bone-side down, on rack of roasting pan. Brush with oil; sprinkle with salt and pepper. Roast at 450 degrees 20 minutes. Reduce heat to 350 degrees, brush turkey with pan juices or caramel sauce (see Cook's Note). Cover with foil and continue roasting 45 minutes or until thermometer registers 170 degrees.

Meanwhile, in heavy saucepan, melt sugar and heat until golden. Add butter and hot water; stir together to make caramel sauce. Place chestnuts, carrots, and garlic cloves in sauce, cover and simmer gently about 10 minutes. Remove chestnuts, carrots and garlic with slotted spoon. Reduce sauce to glazing consistency. Return chestnuts and vegetables.

Remove turkey breast to serving platter. Spoon caramelized chestnuts and vegetables over breast, glazing surface and allowing chestnuts and vegetables to fall and surround turkey.
Yield: 4 to 6 servings

Consider a light, dry,
Pinot Gris or Pinot
Blanc from Oregon.
An Alsatian Tokay
would also complement
this rich and
flavorful
entrée.

Cook's Note: The caramelized chestnuts and vegetables may be prepared ahead and reheated just prior to serving. When prepared ahead you can use a bit of the caramel sauce for basting the turkey breast while roasting.

WONDERFULLY SIMPLE
ROAST TURKEY

10 to 12 pound turkey, preferably fresh
1 onion, peeled and quartered
2 stalks celery, cut into 2-inch lengths
3 to 4 sprigs parsley
2 to 3 tablespoons Herbes de Provence
2 to 3 ounces butter, melted
Salt and freshly ground black pepper

... a turkey that's roasted without being stuffed lends to the excitement of trying totally different dressings on the side.

Remove neck, gizzard, heart, and wing tips. Reserve for making stock. Wash turkey inside and out; pat dry. Place onion, celery and parsley inside turkey along with 1 tablespoon Herbes de Provence, salt and pepper. Truss turkey, if necessary, and brush with some of melted butter. Sprinkle generously with Herbes de Provence, salt, and pepper. Can be done night before and refrigerated, if desired.

Preheat oven to 425 degrees. Oil or spray roasting rack. Place turkey breast-side-down on rack in roasting pan. Place in oven and bake 30 minutes, basting once after 15 minutes. Turn turkey breast-side-up and reduce oven temperature to 325 degrees. Continue roasting and basting with butter or pan juices every 15 to 20 minutes.

Roast approximately 15 to 20 minutes per pound or until meat thermometer registers 170 degrees in thickest part of breast, not touching bone. When done, remove to warm platter. Cover loosely with foil until ready to carve. The dressing of your choice should be baked in a separate casserole dish. Make gravy from defatted pan drippings and stock made from neck and trimmings

Yield: 6 to 8 servings

Although Chardonnay is often the wine of choice here, instead try a J. Fritz Sauvignon Blanc. It's dry, yet lucious, rich and full… a perfect match.

SMITHFIELD HAM
COUNTRY-STYLE

*Don't be afraid to try
this somewhat unusual,
yet traditional, approach
to roasting a country
ham ... cola gives it a
marvelous taste
and color.*

1 (10-pound) joint country or Smithfield ham
4 cups cola soft drink
Whole cloves
1 cup packed dark brown sugar

Soak ham overnight in cold water to remove saltiness. When ready to cook preheat oven to 350 degrees.

Scrub ham well in warm water, removing black pepper and mold. Place in roasting pan. Pour cola over ham, reserving 6 tablespoons.

Roast, uncovered, 2 to 3 hours basting every 20 minutes with pan juices. When internal temperature registers 140 degrees on meat thermometer, remove ham from oven and cool 20 minutes. Increase oven temperature to 375 degrees.

*A cool bone-dry
Tavel Rosé like
Château de
Trinquevedel,
or Beringer's
Rosé de Saginée
will hold the mood
at noon or night.
Both are spicy, exciting
Rosés, typical of those
responsible for the recent
resurgence
of this
category.*

Remove rind from ham with small sharp knife, leaving an even layer of fat. Score fat in diamond pattern to depth of 1/4-inch. Stick a clove in every other diamond. Mix brown sugar and remaining cola. Spread over ham and return ham to oven. Bake 45 minutes, basting with pan juices every 15 minutes. If ham browns too soon, tent loosely with foil. Remove to carving board and rest 15 minutes before carving. Yield: 10 servings

GLAZED BAKED HAM
WITH CRANBERRY MUSTARD

1 (12-pound) partially cooked, bone-in, half ham
2 cups unfiltered apple juice
2 cups water
Whole cloves
1/2 cup honey
1/4 cup bourbon
1/4 cup fresh orange juice
1 cup packed brown sugar
2 tablespoons Dijon mustard
Whole cranberries, sage leaves, and kumquats for garnish

Preheat oven to 350 degrees. Place ham on greased V-rack in 3-inch deep roasting pan. Pour apple juice and water into roasting pan; bake 2 hours. Add more water after first hour if necessary.

Remove ham from oven, trim away skin leaving smooth surface. Score fat diagonally in two directions. Stick clove into each diamond.

To make glaze, mix together honey, bourbon, orange juice, sugar and mustard. Brush glaze over surface of ham and return to oven. Continue to bake 1 hour, basting every 15 minutes with glaze. When done, ham will be golden brown and will register around 130 degrees on meat thermometer.

Transfer ham to platter, tent with foil and let stand 30 minutes. Meanwhile, prepare pan sauce: degrease liquid in roasting pan, add any leftover glaze, and keep warm. Cut ham into 1/4 inch slices; arrange on serving platter and garnish with cranberries, sage and kumquats. Glaze slices with a little of the pan sauce; serve remainder from sauce boat. Serve with Cranberry Mustard on the side.

Yield: 12 servings

Cranberry Mustard
2 cups fresh or frozen cranberries
1 cup water
1/2 cup granulated sugar
2/3 cup Dijon mustard

Place cranberries, water and sugar in sauce pan; cook 5 minutes or until all berries have popped. Cool and mash with a fork to break up; blend into mustard. Serve at room temperature.
Yield: 12 servings

Marvelous when paired with a chilled French or American Viognier. A superb French is Condrieu; an excellent American is the peachy, mellow Viognier from Beringer.

ST. HELENA STEW
OF BLACK-EYED PEAS & HAM

*To ensure good luck and
prosperity in the coming
year, many folks in the
South believe you should
eat black-eyed peas on
New Year's day, perhaps
accompanied by
cornbread and collards.
The peas are said to
stand for pocket change,
the collards for
paper money.*

1 pound dried black-eyed peas, soaked overnight
1 smoked ham hock, blanched 2 minutes
1 cup chopped onion
1 cup chopped green bell pepper
1 cup chopped celery
1 1/2-pounds cooked ham, cut into large cubes
1 bay leaf
8 cups water
2 1/2 tablespoons arrowroot
1 tablespoon Worcestershire sauce
2 tablespoons catsup
Salt to taste
Tabasco sauce to taste
1/2 cup minced parsley
1/2 cup thinly sliced scallion greens
6 cups freshly cooked long grain rice

Drain and rinse peas. Place in kettle with ham hock, onion, bell pepper, celery, ham cubes and bay leaf. Add 8 cups water. Bring to simmer and cook uncovered for 30 minutes, stirring occasionally.

*A rich, mouthfilling
Côtes du Rhone Villages,
like Domaine de la
Renjarde, would
be perfect;
or, if you can find it,
consider a hearty
yet elegant
Stags Leap
Petite Syrah.*

To finish: dissolve arrowroot in small amount of water and stir into stew to thicken juices. Do not boil after addition of arrowroot. Season to taste with Worcestershire, catsup, salt and Tabasco. Transfer to serving dish and garnish with parsley and scallion greens. Serve topped with scoop of freshly cooked rice.

Yield: 8 main dish or 16 cocktail servings

CURRIED ROAST LOIN OF PORK

4 to 5 pound boneless loin of pork roast
2 tablespoons canola oil
1 tablespoon curry powder
1 small onion, peeled and chopped
1 teaspoon ground ginger
1/2 teaspoon ground cardamom
Dash of cayenne pepper
1 1/2 teaspoons salt
1 1/2 cups hot water
2 tablespoons canola oil
2 tablespoons cornstarch, dissolved in
1 cup chicken broth

Tie pork loin at 2 inch intervals with string. Place in covered non-reactive container. Heat canola oil in skillet and sauté curry powder until fragrant and lightly browned. Add onion and continue cooking until onion is softened. Add ginger, cardamom, cayenne and salt. Stir in hot water. Cool and pour over pork loin. Transfer to refrigerator; marinate overnight, turning occasionally.

Preheat oven to 350 degrees. Remove pork loin from marinade and blot dry. Heat canola oil in roasting pan, and brown pork on all sides. Add marinade, bring to simmer, cover and transfer to oven. Roast for 2 1/2 hours basting once or twice. Remove cover and continue roasting 30 minutes.

Remove roast to serving platter; keep warm. Strain pan juices, remove excess fat, and return juices to roasting pan. Add chicken broth mixture to pan juices; whisk over moderate heat until thickened. Taste sauce and adjust seasoning. Slice roast and serve on platter glazed with sauce.
Yield: 6 to 8 servings

Gently flavored with curry, this roast will always delight a family together for the holidays.

Select an Australian Shiraz. Richard Hamilton's Old Vines Reserve made from 105 year old vines, has great balance with rich blackberry and cassis aromas, soft tannins and a long spicy finish.

ROASTED MOCK WILD BOAR
WITH SAUCE GRAND VENEUR

This recipe by Johnee Pinckney won first place in the 1996 Yuletide Recipe contest. "During the 8-day marinating period, expectations for a great feast build each time the ham is turned. It is well worth the wait for that final day when the ham is roasted, carved, and served to eagerly waiting guests."

Mock Wild Boar
1 whole fresh ham (10 to 14 pounds), with rind removed except for a band around the shank

Spice Rub
2 tablespoons ground black pepper
1/2 teaspoon ground thyme
1 teaspoon ground allspice
2 bay leaves, crumbled
1 teaspoon caraway seeds, crushed
1/2 teaspoon celery seed
1/2 teaspoon ground cinnamon
4 tablespoons salt
1 teaspoon grated orange rind
2 tablespoons grated fresh ginger
3 cloves garlic, pressed or minced

Pierce ham with a small knife, making slits over all. Combine ingredients for spice rub and spread by hand, over ham patting until evenly distributed.

Place ham in large plastic bag, and place in ample-sized flat container.

Prepare the marinade.

Marinade
2 medium yellow onions, chopped
1 carrot, peeled and chopped
2 stalks celery, including leaves, chopped
1/2 cup olive oil
1 1/2 cups red wine
1 cup red wine vinegar
1/3 cup brandy

Combine marinade ingredients in saucepan and cook for 5 to 8 minutes. Cool completely and pour over and around ham in the plastic bag. Close bag securely. Place

ham in refrigerator and allow to marinate for at least 8 days or up to 2 weeks. Turn ham twice a day without opening bag.

To Roast: Preheat oven to 300 degrees. Remove ham from bag. (Strain marinade and reserve for sauce.) Do not dry or attempt to remove bits of vegetable which may be clinging to surface. Place ham on rack in roasting pan, fat side up.Roast for 4 1/2 to 5 hours, or until meat thermometer registers 160 to 170 degrees. Allow to rest 20 minutes. Prepare Sauce Grand Veneur while ham is resting.

Sauce Grand Veneur
Strained marinade from ham
2 cups red wine
2 cups beef gravy (or packaged Au Jus mix)
1 cup beef stock (for deglazing roasting pan)
2 to 3 tablespoons currant jelly
1 teaspoon freshly ground black pepper
1 tablespoon finely chopped scallions
2 tablespoons finely chopped parsley
Salt to taste

Combine strained marinade, red wine and beef gravy. Boil over medium heat until mixture is reduced by one-half. (This step can be done at any time during the day.)

After removing ham to carving board, pour excess fat from roasting pan. Bring beef stock to boil, pour into roasting pan and scrape up any browned residue. Add to red wine mixture. Add jelly, pepper, scallions and parsley. Add salt to taste. Add more jelly, if necessary, to balance flavors of wine and vinegar.
Yield: 18 servings

After 8 days in the making, this feast deserves one of the hearty California Zinfandels. It's spicy finish will complement the seasoning and add to the enjoyment.

CANADIAN TOURTIÈRE
WITH WINTER CHILI SAUCE

... originally a pigeon pie which often included ground veal. This version, with pork, is the favorite way it's served in French Canada on Christmas or New Year's Eve.

Either white or red can complement Tourtière ... for a cosmopolitan evening try Australian wines: Four Sisters Sauvignon Blanc with citrus, lime and honey notes, or Billi-Billi, combining Shiraz/Cabernet for lots of spice, pepper and berry with soft tannins.

2 pounds lean ground pork
1 1/2 cups water or beef stock
1 cup finely chopped onion
3 cloves garlic
1 cup finely chopped celery
1 bay leaf
3/4 teaspoon dried savory
1/2 teaspoon freshly ground pepper
1 teaspoon salt
1/4 teaspoon ground cloves
Pinch of cinnamon
Pinch of allspice
1 cup bread crumbs
Pastry for double crust pie

In large shallow pan over medium-high heat, sauté and c[ ] pork until no longer pink. Drain off fat. Add water, onion lic, celery, bay leaf and seasonings; reduce heat and simme[ ] uncovered 30 to 45 minutes or until only 2 tablespoons li[ ] remains. Remove bay leaf, stir in bread crumbs, and adjus[ ] seasoning. Cover and refrigerate until cold.

Preheat oven to 425 degrees. Line 9-inch tin pie plate with try. Spoon in chilled filling and cover with remaining pas[ ] Cut steam vents in top crust and decorate with pastry cut[ ] if desired. Bake for 15 minutes; reduce heat to 375 degree bake 20 to 25 minutes or until crust is golden. Serve in w[ ] with Winter Chili Sauce.
Yield: 8 servings

Winter Chili Sauce

1 (28-ounce) can diced tomatoes in juice
1 large white onion, chopped
1 large Granny Smith apple, peeled, cored, and chopped
1/2 cup chopped celery
1/2 cup chopped green pepper
3/4 cup apple cider vinegar
1 1/4 cups granulated sugar
1/2 teaspoon celery seed
1 teaspoon salt
1/2 teaspoon cinnamon
1/4 teaspoon each black pepper, nutmeg, and ground ginger
Pinch ground cloves
1 tablespoon cornstarch
2 tablespoons water

Make this just once and you'll never again peel tomatoes for a fresh tasting chili sauce! Handy to have on hand for many other meat and egg dishes. When combined with mayonnaise, it also makes a delicious sandwich spread.

Combine all ingredients except cornstarch and water in large non-reactive saucepan. Bring to boil, reduce heat and cook gently about 1 hour or until vegetables are crisp-soft. Stir frequently. Taste and add more spices if necessary to sharpen flavors.

Combine cornstarch and water and add to sauce. Continue cooking until sauce thickens slightly.

If making ahead, ladle into hot sterilized jars and seal. Store in cool place.
Yield: 2 pints

MOUSSAKA MIKANOS

Moussaka is composed of three components which need to be fully prepared before assembling. This hearty and savory dish is a great make-ahead meal for the family's first night home for the holidays.

Eggplant and Potatoes
2 (1-pound) eggplants washed, not peeled
Salt
1/4 cup olive oil, for brushing
2 medium baking potatoes, thinly sliced and simmered until tender

Cut eggplants into 1/2-inch slices. Sprinkle both sides with salt and place in colander about 30 minutes or until beaded with liquid. Blot dry, brush with olive oil and broil 5 minutes on each side until golden. Set aside. Reduce oven temperature to 375 degrees.

Meat Sauce
1 1/2 tablespoons olive oil
1 medium onion, finely chopped
2 cloves garlic crushed or minced
1 1/2 pounds ground lamb (or beef if preferred)
1/2 teaspoon dried oregano
1 teaspoon dried basil
1/2 teaspoon cinnamon
1/2 teaspoon salt
Dash of black pepper
2 (8-ounce) cans tomato sauce

The tannins, oak, and berry of a bold Cabernet Sauvignon pair well with flavorful Moussaka or, from Greece, select a Chateau Carras 30% Cabernet Sauvigon, and 30% Cabernet Franc with Merlot and Limnio. Very nice.

In large frying pan, heat olive oil; add onions and garlic. Sauté 2 to 3 minutes or until onions become translucent. Add ground meat and cook about 10 minutes. Drain in mesh strainer; return to fry-pan. Add oregano, basil, cinnamon, salt, pepper and tomato sauce. Bring to boil, reduce heat and simmer, uncovered, about 10 minutes. Set aside.

Yogurt Topping
3 large eggs, beaten
2 tablespoons flour
2 cups non-fat yogurt
1/2 cup grated Parmigiano-Reggiano cheese

Beat eggs in large bowl. Gradually add flour, mixing well. Add yogurt and stir until smooth.

To assemble: lightly oil 9 x 13-inch baking dish. Layer eggplant and potato mixture with half of meat sauce. Repeat procedure. Any remaining eggplant and potato may be layered on top. Spread the yogurt topping evenly over top; sprinkle with grated cheese. Bake 45 minutes at 375 degrees, or until golden.
Yield: 6 to 8 servings

VEAL & PORK, SAUERKRAUT GOULASH

1 pound lean veal
1 pound lean pork
2 tablespoons vegetable oil
1/2 cup diced onion
1 teaspoon salt
1 teaspoon paprika
1/4 teaspoon pepper
1/2 teaspoon marjoram
1 cup canned diced tomatoes
1 cup penny-sliced carrots
2 1/2 cups canned German sauerkraut packed in wine, undrained
1 cup sour cream

A hearty, traditional German dish has found its way to Lowcountry tables.

Cut meats into 1-inch cubes. Heat oil in large sauté pan; brown meat in batches and remove to side dish. Add onion to pan drippings and sauté 5 minutes. Return browned meats. Add salt, paprika, pepper, marjoram and tomatoes. Cover and simmer 40 to 45 minutes or until meat is tender. Add carrots and sauerkraut. Cook 20 minutes longer. Stir in sour cream just before serving.
Yield: 4 to 6 servings

Delightful with beer, but also enjoyable with a full-bodied, distinctive Gewurtztraminer, or lighter Riesling Kabinet.

KATIE CALLAHAN'S MEATLOAF
WITH SPINACH & CHEDDAR FILLING

On Hilton Head Island, we have a coterie of official "characters". Katie Callahan is one so honored. Her now famous meat loaf may have aided and abetted her legendary status.

2 1/4 pounds meat loaf mix (equal parts ground beef, pork and veal)
2 cups fresh soft bread crumbs
2 eggs lightly beaten
1/2 cup grated Parmigiano-Reggiano cheese
2 tablespoons minced onion
1 teaspoon Italian seasoning, crumbled
1 teaspoon salt
1/4 teaspoon ground black pepper
1/2 cup milk
1 (10-ounce) package frozen spinach, thawed and squeezed dry
1 (8-ounce) package shredded sharp Cheddar cheese, divided

To make meat loaf, place ground meats, bread crumbs, eggs, grated cheese, onion, Italian seasonings, salt, pepper and milk in large bowl. Mix ingredients lightly. Place 12 x 12-inch sheet of plastic wrap on counter. Spread meat loaf mixture on it and pat into 9 x 12-inch rectangle. Spoon spinach over meat to within 1/2-inch of edges. Sprinkle with 1 1/2 cups of the grated Cheddar. Beginning on narrow side, and using plastic wrap to help contour meat loaf, roll jelly-roll style while enveloping the filling.

Katie didn't say, but either a Chilean Merlot or Italian Brunello would help to complete her favorite meatloaf.

Place seam side down in shallow, ungreased baking pan. Bake at 350 degrees about 1 hour and 15 minutes. Remove from oven, sprinkle remaining Cheddar on top; return to oven 5 minutes or until cheese has melted. Remove from oven; let stand 5 minutes until juices settle, before slicing.
Yield: 6 to 8 servings

BOEUF BOURGUIGNON 'NOËL'

1/2 pound thick-sliced bacon, cut into small dice
3 pounds boneless beef chuck, cut into 1-inch cubes
1 cup chopped onions
Salt and freshly ground black pepper, to taste
3 tablespoons all-purpose flour
3 cups good Burgundy wine
3 cups beef stock
2 tablespoons tomato paste
1 tablespoon chopped fresh rosemary leaves
3 to 4 carrots, peeled and cut into 1 1/2 inch julienne
2 cups white pearl onions
8 ounces cremini mushrooms, thickly sliced
1 tablespoon unsalted butter
1 tablespoon red currant jelly
2 tablespoons minced Italian parsley

Preheat oven to 350 degrees. In Dutch oven, sauté bacon until crisp. Pour off all but 1 tablespoon of drippings. Sauté beef, a few pieces at a time, until browned on all sides.

Add chopped onions to beef; sprinkle with salt, pepper and flour. Cook over high heat, stirring constantly, for 5 minutes. Add wine, stock, tomato paste and rosemary. Bring to boil, cover, and transfer to oven. Bake 2 hours, or until meat is tender.

Blanch carrots and onions in boiling water; drain and rinse in cold water. Slip skins off onions. Sauté mushrooms in butter over medium heat. Set aside.

When meat is tender, transfer Dutch oven to burner top. Stir in currant jelly and add prepared vegetables. Serve garnished with minced parsley.
Yield: 8 servings

A Lowcountry adaptation of Burgundy's most famous dish ... just add a crisp salad and good French bread for a memorable fireside supper.

Cook's Note: Always use chuck for the best and most tender stews.

The layers of flavor in a smooth Oregon Pinot Noir, Ponzi for instance, or a Burgundy from the Côtes de Noir, would best suit this classic dish.

GRILLED CHUCK ROAST
STUDEBAKER

*No basting is required
with this method of
grilling, and the meat is
nicely glazed when done.*

5 pound, bone-in, beef chuck roast, 2 1/2 inches thick
Garlic powder
4 cups prepared yellow mustard
3 cups granulated sugar

Sprinkle garlic powder heavily on all surfaces of chuck roast. Place roast in top part of grilling basket. Spread half of mustard on roast. Sprinkle half of sugar over mustard. Attach bottom of grilling basket. Turn grilling basket over exposing other side of roast. Make sure basket is placed over the sink or a drip pan. Repeat layering of mustard and sugar on second side.

Marinate at least 4 hours (6 to 8, if possible) at room temperature. This method of marinating tenderizes the meat.

About an hour before cooking, prepare a very hot charcoal fire. Place grilling basket containing prepared chuck, on grill, directly over heat. Grill about 20 minutes on each side for medium rare, or until meat thermometer registers 130 degrees. Douse any flare-up of flames with water. Do not cook to well-done stage, or meat will be tough. Let stand 10 minutes before carving into thin slices.
Yield: 10 servings

*Open a young red
Crôzes-Hermitage,
Gigondas or Vacqueyras
with this hearty dish.
These Rhône
Appellations are known
for their peppery,
mouth-filling
character.*

SOUTH-OF-THE-BROAD
CRANBERRY POTROAST

1 cup all-purpose flour
1 teaspoon salt
1/2 teaspoon freshly ground black pepper
5 to 6-pound beef rump roast
Vegetable oil for browning roast
1 cup dry red wine
1 stick cinnamon, broken in half
10 whole cloves
2 cups whole cranberries
1 cup water
1/2 cup granulated sugar

The fresh crimson cranberry is part of the beauty of the season. It elevates this simple pot roast to a starring role at Yuletide tables.

Preheat oven to 350 degrees. Combine flour, salt, and pepper. Thoroughly coat roast with the mixture. Over medium-high heat, heat 1/4-inch oil in Dutch oven, add roast and brown on all sides. Add wine, cinnamon and cloves. Cover and roast 3 to 4 hours or until quite tender.

Meanwhile, combine cranberries, water and sugar in sauce pan and cook about 8 minutes or until berries pop.

When roast is tender, remove from oven. Ladle out, and reserve (for Wine Gravy), all pan drippings except for about 1/2-inch. Pour cranberries over roast; return to oven, uncovered, for final 30 minutes. To serve, cut into thick slices topped with cranberries and pan juices. Serve Wine Gravy on the side.

Wine Gravy
Reserved pan drippings
1/4 cup cornstarch
1/2 cup dry red wine
2 cups beef stock
Salt and freshly ground black pepper

If you already have a good red Zinfandel open, keep pouring, especially if it's a Château Souverain… dry, peppery, aged in French oak.

Transfer reserved pan drippings to small saucepan. Combine cornstarch, wine and beef stock; add to pan drippings. Stir over medium heat just until mixture thickens. Season to taste with salt and pepper.

STANDING RIB ROAST AU JUS
WITH YORKSHIRE PUDDING

Two British gastronomic

classics rolled into one ...

the traditional duo of

prime roast beef and

Yorkshire pudding.

For many it's the

number one choice for

Christmas dinner.

1 (8 to 9-pound) standing rib roast, choice or prime, trimmed of excess fat
4 or 5 whole cloves of garlic, peeled
Kitchen string
Salt and freshly ground black pepper

Preheat oven to 325 degrees. Make a few small slits between fat and meat with tip of paring knife; insert garlic cloves. Tie roast at 2 inch intervals with kitchen string. Season roast on all sides with salt and pepper. Arrange roast in roasting pan standing on tips of ribs, creating air pocket underneath. Bake on rack if preferred.

Timing Guideline: Roast 20 minutes for first pound and 15 minutes for each additional pound. Or for 'instant-thermometer' internal reading: 120 for rare, 130 for medium-rare, 135 for medium-well. Temperatures continue to rise during resting period.

When done, remove roast to carving board or platter. Set aside roasting pan and contents; reserve. Tent roast lightly with foil. Place over barely simmering water to keep warm. Increase oven temperature to 400 degrees for Yorkshire Pudding.
Yield: serves 8

Yorkshire Pudding
1 1/2 cups all-purpose flour
3/4 teaspoon salt
3/4 cup milk
3 large eggs, beaten until frothy
3/4 cup water
1/2 cup pan drippings

At least one hour before baking, combine all ingredients (except pan drippings) in bowl of food processor. Process until smooth. Leave mixture in processor. When ready to bake, place 1/2 cup reserved pan drippings, including fat, in 9 x 12-inch baking dish. Heat in oven until very hot. Strain pudding batter directly into hot baking dish. Bake 18 to 20 minutes, reduce temperature to 350 degrees. Continue baking about 10 minutes or until puffed at edges and lightly browned.

Yield: 8 servings

Jus

Remaining drippings in roasting pan
1/2 cup red wine
1 1/2 cups water
4 teaspoons liquid beef concentrate
Salt and pepper, as desired
2 teaspoons cornstarch
1 tablespoon water

Remove as much fat as possible from drippings remaining in roasting pan. Place roasting pan over moderate heat. Pour red wine into pan; boil vigorously while stirring and scraping up all particles. Add 1 1/2 cups water and liquid beef concentrate; continue to boil while stirring to combine. Taste; add salt and pepper as desired. Dissolve cornstarch in water, stir into sauce, and cook until clear.

Yield: 8 servings

Cook's Note: Liquid Beef Concentrate, Beef Base, or Demi-Glace is made by several companies under different names. Do not use bouillon cubes or granules.

This classic deserves a blockbuster red. Look for a West Australian Howard Park Cabernet/Merlot ... loaded with berry, cassis, chocolate, tobacco, and soft plumy fruit. Everyone will be delighted.

BEEF TENDERLOIN STUFFED WITH PORTOBELLO MUSHROOMS

This delicious tenderloin is lean in appearance, and deceptively simple until slicing reveals the riches inside.

4-pound beef tenderloin
1/2 cup butter
1 1/2 pounds portobello mushrooms, chopped
1/2 cup diced celery
3/4 cup diced onion
1 teaspoon salt
1/8 teaspoon black pepper
1/2 teaspoon dried sage
1/2 teaspoon dried thyme
2 tablespoons flour
1 tablespoon garlic olive oil
Salt and pepper to taste
Thick slices of portobellos, brushed with oil
2 tablespoons minced parsley

Preheat oven to 325 degrees. Starting at wide end, slit tenderloin down middle, being careful not to cut through sides. In skillet, melt butter, add mushrooms and sauté until lightly browned. Add celery, onion, salt, pepper, sage and thyme. Sauté until vegetables are tender. Blend in flour and cook 1 minute; cool slightly. Stuff mixture into pocket of beef. Fasten opening with skewers and lace with string. Rub outer surface with garlic olive oil. Season with additional salt and pepper.

Enjoy this with a fine red French Bordeaux or American Cabernet Sauvignon. Serve at room temperature (65 degrees). Chill just slightly if necessary. (The only thing more disappointing than warm red wine is warm white wine!)

Roast tenderloin 20 minutes per pound for medium rare. For garnish: grill portobello slices and place around roast. Sprinkle with minced parsley.
Yield: 10 servings

RACK OF LAMB
WITH HONEY-HAZELNUT CRUST

1 cup ground hazelnuts
1 cup fresh white bread crumbs
3 tablespoons minced fresh rosemary
3 (1 1/2 to 1 3/4-pound) racks of lamb (8-ribs each), trimmed
3 tablespoons Dijon honey mustard
3 tablespoons honey

Preheat oven to 425 degrees. Combine hazelnuts, bread crumbs and rosemary in large bowl. Arrange lamb racks, meat-side-up, in single layer on heavy baking sheet. Brush each rack with 1 tablespoon Dijon honey mustard.

Season each with salt and pepper. Press 2/3 cup bread crumb mixture onto each. Drizzle each lamb rack with 1 tablespoon honey.

Roast about 25 minutes, or until meat thermometer inserted into thickest part of lamb registers 130 degrees for medium-rare. Let lamb stand 10 minutes before carving. Cut between each rib to separate into chops.
Yield: 8 servings

Rack of lamb is a series of connected rib chops. It's a delicious premium cut, and somewhat expensive, yet easy to prepare. This one, with its extraordinary hazelnut crust, could be your pièce de résistance for the entire season.

Lamb pairs well with a hearty Châteauneuf-du-Pape, or, for a delightful change, choose Deakin Shiraz from Australia… soft, jammy, bursting with berry and spice flavors with a nice long finish.

THE LOWCOUNTRY TURKEY FRY

When you serve turkey at Thanksgiving, you are reaching back into time to share a common bond with your ancestors.

When Christopher Columbus came to the New World in 1492, wild turkeys were here to greet him. And we suppose native Americans around the Plymouth Colony in 1621 actually did show up with a few wild gobblers for that first Thanksgiving feast. It is believed that Squanto and his friends boiled them in huge pots over open fires.

Wild turkeys were abundant on Hilton Head until the Charles Fraser development years in the 1960's. Even today an occasional one is sighted crossing highway 278 in the vicinity of Hilton Head Plantation.

But it's how we cook them here that makes the difference – and not just for Thanksgiving, but at beach picnics and for polo tailgating.We like them deep-fried! We're back to that original pot method where we cook them whole, but this time around in a pot of bubbling oil.

The process begins the day before the feast. Wash and pat dry the turkey; trim the fat around the neck and tail; cut open the neck to make sure the oil can circulate through the turkey.

The turkey is seasoned inside and out with dry Creole-Cajun spices. Double wrapped to keep in the powerful scent of spices, the turkey marinates overnight in the refrigerator. Local Island pit master Elgie Stover injects his turkeys with a special concoction at this point ... an option.

The following day Islanders set up a portable propane stove, fill a 60-quart pot with around six gallons of peanut oil, and tie the turkey with string to keep wings tucked in. When oil reaches 375 degrees the turkey, in a huge fry basket, is lowered into the hot oil. The fat churns like a geyser around the bird.

Frying takes 3 to 4 minutes per pound, which means a seventeen pound turkey can be ready in about an hour. The perfectly browned skin is crisp and sinful. It's gone in minutes.

$\mathscr{S}$EASONAL VEGETABLES & SIDES

It takes a delicious variety

of side dishes to make holiday menus complete.

Whether you prefer traditional sides

or something other than the norm,

our collection is sure to please.

They are tasty and attractive

and go well with any holiday main course.

Some of these side dishes are so outstanding,

they could almost serve as a centerpiece.

ARTICHOKE SOUFFLÉ
WITH SHERRY SAUCE

2 (10 1/2-ounce) packages frozen artichoke hearts
Salted water, to cover
3 eggs, plus 3 egg yolks
2 cups heavy cream
1/4 teaspoon salt
Pinch ground white pepper, or to taste
1 teaspoon sugar
2 teaspoons rose water
1/2 cup sherry
2 tablespoons butter

Everyone likes to serve souffés at their highest peak. Actually, height is not as important as texture and flavor, and recognizing the best effort of the cook!

Preheat oven to 375 degrees. Butter a 6-cup soufflé dish; set aside. Meanwhile, boil artichoke hearts in salted water to cover until very soft; purée them in food processor. Set aside.

In large mixer bowl, beat eggs and yolks well. Add cream, salt, pepper, sugar and rose water. Continue beating until foamy; fold in puréed artichoke hearts. Spoon into prepared soufflé dish. Place soufflé dish in hot water bath and bake for 45 minutes or until set.

While soufflé is baking, prepare sauce. Heat sherry in small sauce pan; whisk in 2 tablespoons butter. Serve warm from a sauce boat.

Yield: 8 servings

SCALLOPED BLUFFTON OYSTERS

A local delicacy, oysters were once a major attraction for nomadic people living among the barrier islands. A large shell ring left around a temporary village can still be visited in Sea Pines. Bluffton oysters are considered a rare treat in these parts.

2 pints fresh shucked Bluffton oysters
8 tablespoons melted butter
1 tablespoon lemon juice
2 cups coarsely crumbled saltine crackers
Freshly ground black pepper
1/2 pint half and half
1/2 teaspoon salt
1/3 teaspoon Worcestershire sauce
1 teaspoon sherry

Preheat oven to 350 degrees. Butter a 6-cup baking dish. Drain oysters, reserving liquid. Combine butter and lemon juice. Pour over cracker crumbs, tossing to mix.

In prepared baking dish, layer 1/3 crumbs and half of oysters. Repeat 1/3 crumbs and remaining oysters. Sprinkle oysters lightly with pepper. Combine reserved oyster liquid with enough half and half to make one cup. Stir in salt, Worcestershire and sherry. Pour over oysters. Top with remaining 1/3 crumb mixture. Bake 30 minutes or until thoroughly heated. Yield: 6 servings

14-CARROT CHEDDAR RING

2 pounds carrots, peeled and chopped
Salted water to cover
1 cup fresh bread crumbs
1 cup milk
3/4 cup grated sharp Cheddar cheese
1/2 cup melted butter
1/4 cup grated onion
1 teaspoon salt
1/4 teaspoon black pepper
3 eggs
2 tablespoons grated Parmigiano-Reggiano cheese

Add color as well as flavor with this delicious make-now, bake-later vegetable ... a lovely presentation when the center is filled with green peas or sautéed mushroom caps.

Preheat oven to 350 degrees; spray a non-stick 6 cup ring mold and set aside.

Cook carrots in salted water until very tender. Drain; place in bowl of food processor and process until puréed. Return to mixing bowl; add remaining ingredients, except eggs and cheese. Stir to combine well. Beat eggs until light and fluffy; fold into carrot mixture. Spoon into prepared ring mold. (May be held at this point and baked later.)

Place ring mold in hot-water bath, tent with foil and bake at 350 degrees for 45 minutes. Remove tent and sprinkle top with grated cheese. Return to oven for another 10 minutes. Cool 5 minutes before unmolding onto warm plate.
Yield: 8 servings

GEECHEE SMASHED RUTABAGA

4 pounds rutabaga, peeled, cut into 1/2-inch dice
2 tablespoons brown sugar
6 tablespoons butter, or part butter and part light cream
Salt and freshly ground pepper to taste

Drop diced rutagaga into lightly salted boiling water to cover; reduce to simmer, cover and cook 15 to 20 minutes or until tender. Drain thoroughly and mash with brown sugar. Add butter or butter and cream. Season to taste with salt and pepper.
Yield: 8 servings

Cook's Note: Taste a raw piece of rutabaga. If it is slightly bitter, use skim milk in place of water for cooking.

Some call this vegetable

a baggy root;

we call

it delicious!

Geechee and Gullah

are synonymous.

BRAISED RED CABBAGE

1 small head red cabbage
4 bay leaves
Small onion studded with 6 whole cloves
2 Granny Smith apples, peeled, cored, and diced
1 cup apple juice
Dash of cider vinegar
Salt and pepper, to taste

Quarter and core cabbage. Shred cabbage and place in heavy-gauge, non-reactive covered pot. Add bay leaves, onion studded with cloves and apples. Braise covered, over moderate heat for approximately 1 hour.

Meanwhile, simmer apple juice until reduced to 1/2 cup and stir into cabbage. During last 10 minutes remove and discard bay leaves and studded onion. Add dash of vinegar to preserve color. Taste cabbage and adjust seasoning with salt and pepper.
Yield: 6 servings

A winning flavor to

combine with all kinds of

roasted meats, especially

pork and game.

ACORN SQUASH
WITH WILD RICE & PECANS

4 small acorn squash

8 tablespoons butter

8 tablespoons brown sugar

Salt and pepper

3 cups chicken broth

1 cup wild rice

1/2 cup raisins

1 tablespoon dried basil

1/3 cup chopped pecans, lightly toasted

A surprisingly delightful blend of winter flavors… refreshing on a chilly holiday evening.

Preheat oven to 350 degrees. Cut acorn squash in half crosswise and scoop out seeds. Shave off pointed ends so each half can sit flat in pan. Place cut-side-down in shallow baking dish. Gently pour about one inch of boiling water into dish. Bake for 45 minutes.

Turn cut-side-up. Into each cavity put 1 tablespoon each butter and brown sugar. Sprinkle with salt and freshly ground black pepper. Bake 15 minutes longer.

While squash is baking, prepare wild rice. Bring broth to boil. Add wild rice, cover and simmer 30 minutes. Add raisins and basil; simmer 15 minutes more, or until rice is tender. Toss with pecans. Divide rice mixture among cavities of cooked squash. Serve at once.

Yield: 8 servings

GRATIN OF WINTER
ROOT VEGETABLES

Vermouth is the surprising ingredient in this winter vegetable gratin… it definitely elevates the flavors.

2 tablespoons butter

1 large onion, chopped

1 pound russet potatoes, peeled, thinly sliced

1 pound yams, peeled, thinly sliced

1 (8-ounce) turnip, peeled, thinly sliced

1 cup canned chicken broth

1 cup dry vermouth

Salt and black pepper, to taste

Preheat oven to 375 degrees. Butter an 8 x 8-inch baking dish with 2-inch sides; set aside. Melt butter in large heavy saucepan over medium heat. Add onion and sauté about 8 minutes, or until tender. Add potatoes, yams, turnip, stock and vermouth. Season generously with salt and pepper. Stir gently until liquid comes to boil. Transfer vegetables and liquid to prepared dish. Bake about one hour, or until vegetables are tender and most of liquid is absorbed. Let stand ten minutes before serving.

Yield: 6 to 8 servings

GREEN BEAN & VIDALIA ONION GRATINÉE

2 pounds whole green beans
2 pounds small Vidalia onions
6 tablespoons butter
6 tablespoons all-purpose flour
1 teaspoon salt
1/4 teaspoon nutmeg
3/4 teaspoon white pepper
4 1/2 cups chicken stock
1 1/2 cups half and half cream
Crumb topping
2 cups fresh French bread crumbs
2 to 3 tablespoons grated Parmigiano-Reggiano cheese
2 tablespoons extra-virgin olive oil

Preheat oven to 350 degrees. Trim green beans; cut into 1 inch lengths and blanch about 4 minutes. Drain and plunge into ice-water to cool. Peel onions; cut into 1/2-inch slices. Place in flat container of boiling water. Simmer gently 3 or 4 minutes, drain, plunge into ice water and break into rings.

For sauce, melt butter in saucepan and add flour. Cook one minute without browning. Stir in salt, nutmeg and white pepper. Whisk in chicken stock. When thickened, whisk in cream.

Layer half of green beans in buttered 9 x 13-inch baking dish; spoon over one-fourth of sauce. Layer half of onions over green beans followed by one-fourth of sauce. Repeat layering, ending with onions on top. Spoon over remaining sauce. Combine crumbs and grated cheese, drizzle with olive oil and spread on top of dish. Tent loosely with foil.

Bake 35 minutes or until bubbling. Remove tent after 20 minutes to brown crumbs.
Yield: 8 to 10 servings

A southern comfort dish that is a far cry from the classic Green Bean Bake developed years ago. Here we use local Vidalia onions, tender fresh green beans, and a creamy homemade sauce. It has become a Thanksgiving dinner staple wherever you live. It varies regionally.

SPROUTS & CHESTNUTS

"As a bride, I thought

the chestnuts on the tree

outside our home would

be just fine for cooking.

Fortunately, I tasted one

before adding them to

the sprouts. Surprise,

surprise! They were

bitter horse chestnuts!"

1 1/2 pounds Brussels sprouts, washed and trimmed
4 tablespoons unsalted butter
3/4 pound chestnuts, peeled and cooked, see
Cook's Note
Salt and pepper to taste
Nutmeg to taste

Cut an 'x' in base of each Brussels sprout, drop into boiling salted water to cover and cook, uncovered, 4 to 10 minutes or until just barely tender. Plunge into ice-water for a few seconds to stop cooking and set color. Drain and set aside.

In same saucepan, melt butter over med-low heat; sauté chestnuts 5 minutes or until golden. Add Brussels sprouts to chestnuts, season to taste, and cook, partially covered, about 3 minutes. Shake pan occasionally to prevent uneven browning.
Yield: 8 servings

Cook's Note: To prepare chestnuts: cut a cross in flat side of each deep enough to cut through skin and pierce inner flesh. Drop into boiling water for 3 to 5 minutes. Remove and drain. Insert tip of paring knife into slit and peel away skin including brown inner skin. Place nuts in saucepan and pour boiling water over. Cover and simmer for about 30 minutes or until chestnuts are tender but not mushy. Drain. Proceed as above.

CAULIFLOWER &
BROCCOLI DOME

1 large head cauliflower, broken into flowerets
1 1/2-pound bunch broccoli, broken into flowerets,
and stems peeled
6 tablespoons butter, melted
1 cup fresh bread crumbs
2 tablespoons fresh lemon juice
Salt and freshly ground pepper, to taste

This attractive vegetable presentation will add color and balance to almost any festive dinner... and is really quite easy to assemble.

Butter or spray an 8-inch oven-proof bowl, 5 to 6 inches deep. Set aside. Drop cauliflower into boiling salted water 5 minutes or until crisp tender. Remove with slotted spoon and plunge into ice water. In same pot, cook broccoli 3 to 5 minutes and cool as for cauliflower. Drain both vegetables.

Arrange most uniform flowerets (heads down, stems pointing inward), snugly against one another in oiled bowl, alternating colors of white and green. Fill in center with stems and smaller pieces. Gently press downward to flatten top. Press buttered foil on top of vegetables. May refrigerate at this point.

Preheat oven to 300 degrees. Bake dish 15 to 18 minutes or until heated. Meanwhile, melt butter and brown bread crumbs.

To serve: remove foil, place serving plate on bowl, and invert to unmold. Drizzle with lemon juice. Season with salt and pepper and pat crumbs evenly over dome.
Yield: 8 servings

MEDLEY OF MINTED VEGETABLES

Fortunately, mint grows almost year 'round in South Carolina. Other root vegetables such as parsnips or rutabagas may be used instead of, or in addition to, the carrots.

Cook's Note: If the vegetables are tender before all liquid has evaporated, pour off remaining liquid before glazing with butter and garnishing with mint.

3 medium carrots, peeled
1 cucumber, peeled
1 zucchini
1/2 cup water
1 teaspoon sugar
Pinch salt
1 1/2 tablespoons butter, cubed
1 tablespoon coarsely chopped fresh mint leaves

Cut carrots, cucumbers, and zucchini into 2 1/2x1/2-inch sticks.

Combine carrots, water, sugar and salt in medium saucepan. Cover, bring to boil and simmer about 5 minutes. Increase heat; add cucumber and zucchini. Continue cooking until all vegetables are tender-crisp and liquid has completely evaporated. Add butter and chopped mint. Stir to glaze vegetables with butter and distribute mint evenly.
Yield: 4 to 6 servings

CARAMELIZED NEW POTATOES

To caramelize potatoes, an electric wok also works extremely well. Melt sugar and caramelize it at 375 degrees. Reduce heat to 300 degrees, add butter and potatoes. Turn potatoes to coat evenly. The wok accommodates larger numbers of potatoes at one time.

24 small new potatoes, unpeeled
Salted water to cover
1/2 cup granulated sugar
1/4 pound butter, melted

Boil new potatoes in salted water to cover about 20 minutes, or until tender. Cool and remove skins.

Heat sugar in heavy 10 to 12-inch frying pan over low heat. Cook until sugar melts, caramelizes, and turns light brown in color. Stir in melted butter and as many potatoes as possible without crowding pan. Shake pan constantly, rolling potatoes until evenly coated with caramel. Remove to side dish and keep warm. Repeat process with remaining potatoes until all are coated.
Yield: 8 servings

POMMES DE TERRE BOURSIN

3 1/2 pounds potatoes, peeled and cut into 2-inch chunks
Salted water to cover
2 (5-ounce) packages Boursin cheese with herbs and garlic
1/2 cup half and half cream
Salt and freshly ground pepper to taste

Cook potatoes in boiling salted water, to cover, 20 to 25 minutes or until very tender. Drain in colander and return to pot. Cook over low heat briefly to evaporate any excess water.

Preheat oven to 350 degrees. With a hand held mixer, beat potatoes until smooth. Cut Boursin into chunks and add to potatoes, continuing to beat until blended. Add half and half to reach desired consistency. Season to taste with salt and pepper. Transfer to ovenproof casserole and bake, uncovered, until piping hot.
Yield: 8 servings

Cook's Note: If Boursin cheese is not available, here is a mock version you can create in minutes: blend 1 (8-ounce) package cream cheese, a finely minced garlic clove, 1/2 cup softened butter, 2 teaspoons Herbes de Provence and a dash of Tabasco sauce. Mix well and refrigerate several hours before serving.

This mashed potato dish steals the show no matter when it's served. When the recipe appeared in a Thanksgiving menu published in the Island Packet, in no time there wasn't a package of Boursin cheese left on the Island.

ROASTED GARLIC
MASHED POTATOES

Roasted garlic elevates potatoes to a celestial plane! It also does wonders for rice, salad dressings, soups, and vegetable dishes, or simply spread on good crusty bread.

4 pounds medium all-purpose potatoes, peeled and quartered
Salted water to cover
1 cup whole milk or half and half, heated
6 tablespoons unsalted butter at room temperature
Pulp from 2 heads roasted garlic, mashed
Salt and freshly ground pepper, to taste

Boil potatoes in salted water to cover about 20 minutes, or until tender. Drain and return to heat briefly, shaking pan to remove any excess moisture. Mash potatoes by hand or with electric mixer (not in Food Processor) until reasonably smooth. Add milk slowly, beating to desired consistency. Beat in butter and roasted garlic (recipe follows). Season to taste with salt and pepper. Serve immediately.
Yield: 8 servings

Roasted Garlic
1 teaspoon olive oil
2 large heads garlic, with 1/4-inch trimmed off top to expose tops of cloves

Remove parchment-like skin that can easily be pulled away from garlic. Place in baking dish, cut side up. Brush lightly with olive oil, cover with foil, and bake at 375 degrees 50 to 60 minutes, or until garlic feels soft when gently pressed. Cool slightly before turning heads upside down and squeezing gently to remove pulp from skins.

For a stronger roasted flavor, place garlic cut side down on a foil lined baking sheet. Roast at 400 degrees 45 to 50 minutes, or until tender.

LOWCOUNTRY SWEET POTATOES

2 (16-ounce) cans sweet potatoes, drained
1/4 cup butter, softened
1/2 cup granulated sugar
2 eggs, beaten
1/2 cup light cream
1 teaspoon vanilla extract
Several grindings fresh nutmeg
1/8 teaspoon salt
Praline topping (see sidebar)

Preheat oven to 350 degrees and butter 8-cup shallow baking dish. Mash sweet potatoes and add all other ingredients. Mix well. Spoon mixture into prepared baking dish. Spread praline topping evenly over sweet potatoes. Bake 25 to 30 minutes.
Yield: 8 servings

Praline Topping
1/2 cup brown sugar, packed to measure
3 tablespoons flour
1/4 cup butter, softened
1/2 cup chopped pecans

Combine all ingredients and mix well.

MASHED AMARETTO SWEET POTATOES

6 large sweet potatoes, peeled, and cubed
Salted water to cover
4 tablespoons butter, softened
3 tablespoons Amaretto liqueur
3 tablespoons whipping cream
Pinch of salt (or to taste)
2 tablespoons sliced almonds, toasted
Optional garnish, dollops of whipped cream

Boil sweet potatoes in salted water to cover. When tender, drain and transfer to large mixing bowl. Mash potatoes while adding butter, Amaretto, whipping cream and salt. Spoon into serving dish, and garnish top with toasted sliced almonds and, if desired, dollops of whipped cream.
Yield: 8 servings

Sweet potatoes and Amaretto were made for each other ... the proof is in this pudding.

I CAN'T BELIEVE IT'S GRITS

Every one loves grits in the South. This rendition isn't traditional but it is a contemporary adaptation.

1 quart milk
1 stick butter, cut into cubes
1 cup quick-cooking grits (not instant)
1 teaspoon salt
1/8 teaspoon freshly ground pepper
1/3 cup melted butter
1/2 cup, plus 2 tablespoons freshly grated
Parmigiano-Reggiano cheese

In heavy saucepan bring milk to boiling and add butter. Over moderate heat gradually stir in grits until mixture is thickened. Simmer 5 minutes, stirring frequently. Off heat, add salt and pepper. Beat with electric beaters 5 minutes or until grits have developed a creamy consistency. Pour into 9 x 9-inch dish. Chill until set.

Preheat oven to 375 degrees. Lightly butter a second 9 x 9-inch baking dish.

Slice chilled grits into 1 1/2 x 2-inch rectangles; arrange in slightly overlapping rows in prepared baking dish. Pour melted butter over tops and sprinkle with grated cheese. Bake, tented with foil, 35 minutes. Remove tent last 10 minutes and allow tops to brown lightly.
Yield: 6 servings

APPLE RAISIN PILAF

2 tablespoons butter
1 small onion, chopped
1 cup long grain rice
2 cups apple juice
1 baking apple, peeled, cored and sliced
1/2 cup raisins
1 teaspoon cinnamon

Melt butter in sauté pan. Sauté onion briefly. Add rice and continue sautéing until rice is golden brown. Add apple juice, apple, raisins and cinnamon. Simmer, covered, over low heat about 15 minutes or until liquid is absorbed. Transfer to serving dish and serve while steaming hot.
Yield: 6 servings

This unusual pilaf is exceptionally good when served with roast pork, duck, and game dishes. The richness is nicely balanced by the flavors of fruit and spice ... leftovers make a wonderful rice pudding.

BAKED APPLES FILLED WITH CHUTNEY

8 medium baking apples, such as Rome Beauty
4 teaspoons fresh lemon juice
1 1/2 cups mango or cranberry chutney

Preheat oven to 375 degrees. Cut about 1/2 inch from top of each apple. Remove cores to provide generous cavities. Brush cavities with lemon juice and fill with chutney. Arrange in baking pan, cover loosely with foil, and pour 1/2 inch of water around apples. Bake for 35 minutes. Remove foil, and place under broiler until tops are bubbly and caramelized.
Yield: 8 servings

…another unusual side dish, great with roasted pork or poultry… especially well-suited to those flavored with curry.

WILD PECAN RICE DRESSING

The ingredient list just looks intimidating …actually this dressing goes together very easily and can be prepared the day before.

1 (7-ounce) box Wild Pecan Rice
3/4 cup wild rice
2 (14 1/2-ounce) cans chicken broth
1/4 cup unsalted butter or oil
2 cups diced onion
1 1/2 cups diced celery
2 tart apples, peeled, cored and diced
1 tablespoon fresh thyme or 1 teaspoon dried
1 teaspoon fresh sage or 1/2 teaspoon dried
1/4 teaspoon each allspice and paprika
Freshly ground black pepper
Pinch cayenne
1/2 cup coarsely broken pecans, toasted
3/4 cup dried cranberries
1/3 cup chopped parsley
Zest and juice of 1 orange

Cook Wild Pecan Rice in 1 can chicken broth plus 3 tablespoons water, 20 to 25 minutes or until stock is absorbed and rice is tender.

Cook wild rice in second can of chicken broth 45 to 50 minutes or until rice is tender. (Add more water if necessary.)

Heat butter or oil in large frying pan; add onion, celery, apple, and seasonings. Sauté 5 to 8 minutes, stirring frequently, until vegetables are tender. Stir in pecans, cranberries, parsley, orange zest, juice and the cooked rice mixtures. Mix well and adjust seasoning. Spoon into oven-proof serving dish. Bake at 350 degrees for 15 to 20 minutes or until heated through.

May be refrigerated overnight, in which case, bring to room temperature and reheat, covered, 20 to 25 minutes at 350 degrees. Uncover last 5 minutes.
Yield: 12 servings

TRADITIONAL CORNBREAD DRESSING

5 quarts crumbled dried cornbread
2 quarts crumbled dried biscuits
3 1/2 teaspoons dried thyme
2 1/2 teaspoons dry rubbed sage
1/4 cup butter
4 cups roughly chopped onion
4 cups roughly chopped celery
4 eggs, slightly beaten
4 quarts canned chicken broth, or homemade stock
Salt and pepper, to taste

Place cornbread and biscuit crumbs in large mixing bowl. Add thyme and sage and toss together. Melt butter in large fry pan. Sauté onion and celery until beginning to brown. Add to bread mixture. Stir beaten eggs into bread mixture. Heat stock to boiling and pour over bread mixture, stirring until desired consistency is reached. Taste, and add salt and pepper as desired.

The dressing may be used to stuff the turkey, or baked and served as a side dish. Recipe may easily be cut in half. It freezes well.

Cook's Note: Three 9-inch pans of cornbread will yield about 5 quarts of crumbs. It is best to bake cornbread and biscuits a day or two ahead and let them dry a bit. Or, after crumbling by hand or in food processor, they may be dried in a 250 degree oven. Biscuits may be made from refrigerated biscuit products.
Yield: 16 servings, with possibility of leftovers

"I've never had a written recipe for our family cornbread stuffing. My grandmother, mother, and I have just learned by watching and tasting. For this cookbook, I've measured and written down the ingredients. Now I can share it with all of you."

CALIBOGUE OYSTER STUFFING

Simple herbed oyster stuffing is standard holiday fare for many Islanders ... natives and transplants alike.

8 cups toasted bread cubes
1/2 pound butter
1 cup finely chopped shallots
1 quart oysters, with their liquor
1 tablespoon fresh tarragon, or 2 teaspoons dry, refreshed in white wine
1 cup finely chopped parsley
1 tablespoon salt
1 1/2 teaspoons freshly ground pepper

To make bread crumbs, cut good-quality firm white bread into small cubes. Toast in oven at 325 degrees for 20 minutes, stirring once or twice.

Heat butter in heavy skillet over medium heat and sauté shallots until softened. Add bread cubes and stir until all butter is absorbed. Add oysters and their liquor. Combine remainder of ingredients; add to bread cube mixture and toss well. Taste and correct seasoning.
Yield: stuffing for a 10-pound turkey

Cook's Note: To estimate amount of stuffing needed for the turkey allow 1 cup per pound.

MOTHER'S PIONEER DRESSING

8 to 10 cups crustless bread, diced
4 cups chopped onion
2 cups chopped celery
1 cup chopped fresh parsley
1 1/2 teaspoons salt
1 teaspoon ground nutmeg
1/4 cup fresh sage leaves, chopped or
1 tablespoon dry rubbed sage
1 1/2 cups chopped walnuts
3/4 pound butter melted
2 cups chicken broth, or more if needed

Mix together all ingredients except butter and broth. When bread mixture is well combined add butter. Add chicken broth sufficient to moisten bread; mixture should not be too wet. Spoon into buttered 2-quart casserole. Bake, tented with foil, along with the turkey during the last 50 minutes of roasting time.
Yield: 12 to 14 servings

"My mother's timeless Pioneer Dressing was inherited from Grandma Burt. It was passed to her from Great Grandma Howard, who probably made it first, and brought it along when she and Great Grandpa crossed the plains in a Conestoga wagon heading for Utah."

SOUTHERN AMBROSIA

6 oranges, peeled and seeded
1 fresh golden pineapple, peeled and cored
1 cup grated fresh or frozen coconut
1/3 cup granulated sugar
2 1/2 tablespoons dry sherry

Cut oranges and pineapple into 1/2-inch chunks. Combine with coconut, sugar and sherry. Cover and chill at least 4 hours.
Yield: 8 servings

Cook's Note: Frozen coconut is now available in the frozen food section of supermarkets

Southerners often speak reverently when discussing ambrosia. In mythology it means fruit of the gods, yet it is a down-to-earth dish. No self-respecting Hilton Head holiday table would be without it.

page 115

THE COASTAL ENVIRONMENT

To sustain our heritage for generations to come, Islanders know they must preserve their environment.

Coastal Discovery, the Environmental and Historical Museum on Hilton Head Island, over the past dozen years, has grown to become a treasured Island center for exploring the unique coastal ecology and history of the sea islands and Lowcountry.

This is a hands-on museum with artifacts and specimens of native American pottery and stone implements, remnants of the Civil War, and natural history specimens.

On-site nature walks and history tours are made to our beaches, marsh areas, Civil War history sites, native American archeological dig areas, and sea island plantation sites. From pre-school to the adult and senior community, the museum is a great experience.

The Coastal Discovery Museum is active in the preservation of Island resources, both natural and historical. It sponsors educational activities like the Sea Turtle Protection Project, The Dolphin Project, and the South Carolina Beach Sweep.

Hidden down on the Island's toe in Sea Pines is the on-going preservation of the Stoney Baynard Ruins. The great Baynard house was built of tabby around 1793 by Captain John Stoney as part of Braddocks Point Plantation. The Stoney family became the most powerful family on the Island, and at one point owned a vast majority of the land through one branch of the family or other.

This house remained in the Stoney family until the fateful night in the 1830's when William Edings Baynard entered into a high stakes poker game. Legend has it that when the game ended, Baynard owned the Great Braddocks Point Plantation house, dock, land, slaves, and all. Some say he got it all with a pair of Kings!

Friends of Stoney Baynard Ruins, founded by Jane Plante, has sponsored archeological research and digs at this site at Plantation and Baynard Parks Roads to better understand this 19th century way of life.

 CRANBERRIES À LA CARTE

*In 1677 cranberries were
said to be the 'choicest product of the colony'
and were one of the first native fruits to be
shipped to Europe commercially.
More than 300 years later
their popularity continues to soar.*

*The flavor of cranberries, like the flavor of lemons,
has a universal appeal in all aspects of the menu,
from beverages and appetizers
through entrées and desserts – as well as in relishes,
chutneys, and condiments – so much so, that we have
devoted this chapter to them.
May you thoroughly
enjoy Cranberries à la Carte!*

FROSTED CRANBERRIES

12 ounces fresh cranberries, picked over and washed
1 egg white
1/2 cup granulated sugar

After washing cranberries, roll in kitchen towels to dry.
Beat egg white until fluffy. Spread sugar on bottom
surface of a pie tin. Dip cranberries, a few at a time,
into beaten egg white. Transfer to pie tin and roll them
around gently until well coated with sugar. Transfer
onto waxed paper until set.

Cook's Note: Pasteurized eggs or egg beaters may be
substituted for egg white, if there is a concern about
serving uncooked egg white.

This confection is dazzling and elegant and easy to make. Heap them in a glass bowl on the coffee table and watch them disappear.

CRANBERRY EGG NOG FOR CAROLERS

1 quart ready-prepared dairy eggnog
1 (32-ounce) bottle cranberry juice, chilled
2 cups heavy cream, chilled and whipped with
2 tablespoons granulated sugar
Dash ground cloves

Place eggnog in chilled punch bowl. Stir in cranberry
juice. Fold in whipped cream. Serve in punch cups
topped with a dash of cloves.
Yield: 10 servings

Sometimes called Bog Nog where cranberries grow, eggnog made with cranberry juice can be served to carolers as a special treat.

HOT BUTTERED CRANBERRY PUNCH

... using a cinnamon stick as a stirrer imparts flavor and enhances the aroma of this spicy hot beverage.

2/3 cup brown sugar, firmly packed
1/4 teaspoon salt
1/2 teaspoon ground cinnamon
1/2 teaspoon ground allspice
1/4 teaspoon freshly ground nutmeg
3/4 teaspoon ground cloves
4 cups water
2 (1-pound) cans jellied cranberry sauce
4 cups canned pineapple juice
Butter
Whole cinnamon sticks for stirrers

To make spiced syrup: mix brown sugar, salt and spices with 1 cup of water in a saucepan. Bring to boil, stirring until sugar dissolves.

In large non-reactive saucepan, crush cranberry sauce with a fork and add remaining 3 cups water, pineapple juice and spiced syrup. Over moderate heat bring to simmer, stirring frequently. Continue to simmer 5 minutes.

To serve, ladle into mugs and top with dot of butter. Stand a cinnamon stick in each mug.
Yield: 20 servings

Cook's Note: Acidic foods, like cranberries, may react negatively with ordinary aluminum cookware, tin-lined copper, or untreated iron ware. Non-reactive cookware such as stainless steel, enameled steel, or anodized aluminum is now preferred in the kitchen.

CURRIED CRANBERRY CHUTNEY

1 3/4 cups granulated sugar
1 3/4 cups water
4 cups fresh cranberries, washed and picked over
1 cup golden raisins
1 1/2 tablespoons curry powder
2 teaspoons ground ginger
1/2 teaspoon ground nutmeg
2 tablespoons molasses
1 teaspoon salt
1 tablespoon Worcestershire sauce
1/2 teaspoon Tabasco sauce

Cranberry season is short, but you can freeze these crimson gems right in their original bags for up to a year. This is the time of the year to stock up. This chutney is wonderful during Yuletide and throughout the year.

Combine sugar and water in large non-reactive pan. Bring to boil, stirring until sugar is dissolved. Reduce heat and simmer 5 minutes. Add cranberries; simmer uncovered, stirring occasionally, 8 minutes or until skins pop. Stir in raisins and remaining ingredients. Continue simmering, uncovered, about 25 minutes or until mixture has begun to thicken. Spoon chutney into sterilized jars, filling to within 1/2-inch of top. Wipe jar rims and cover with metal lids and screw-on bands. Refrigerate after opening.
Yield: 4 half-pint jars

CRANBERRY-PEAR CHUTNEY

An unusual chutney with a very nice Asian flair through the addition of ginger and garlic.

3/4 cup cider vinegar
1 1/2 cups light brown sugar
1 (12-ounce) bag fresh cranberries
1 1/2 cups peeled, cored and chopped pears
1 small garlic clove, peeled and minced
1/2 teaspoon minced fresh ginger root
1/2 teaspoon salt
Pinch cayenne pepper
3 slices fresh lemon, seeds removed

Bring vinegar and sugar to boil; add fruits and reduce heat to simmer. Add remaining ingredients, except lemon slices. Continue simmering 10 minutes, or until fruit is soft. Add lemon slices last; cook about 2 minutes. Spoon into sterilized half-pint jars; place lemon slice in each. Cap and store in cool place.
Yield: 3 half-pint jars

PIQUANT CRANBERRY CONSERVE

Turkey or game is much enhanced by the spiciness of this conserve.

1 pound fresh cranberries, washed and picked over
3/4 cup cider vinegar
1/2 cup water
1 (2-inch) piece fresh ginger root
1 stick cinnamon
1 teaspoon whole allspice
6 whole cloves
Small square cheesecloth
1 1/2 cups brown sugar

Place cranberries in non-reactive saucepan. Add vinegar and water. Tie ginger, cinnamon, allspice, and cloves in cheesecloth and drop into cranberries. Bring to boil, lower heat, and simmer until skins pop. Add sugar and continue simmering 20 minutes, stirring frequently. Remove spice bundle. Spoon conserve into hot, sterilized half-pint jars and seal. Refrigerate until needed.
Yield: 3 half-pint jars

CRANBERRY VINEGAR

4 cups chopped fresh cranberries
2 cups champagne or white wine vinegar
16 fresh plump cranberries
2 (8-inch) bamboo skewers
2 (8-ounce) bottles, sterilized

Place chopped cranberries in non-reactive container such as a large glass jar or crock. Pour 2 cups vinegar over them, possibly a little more to make sure they are completely covered. Store at cool room temperature for 4 to 10 days. Taste after 4 days and each day thereafter until flavor has sufficiently developed.

When ready to bottle, strain mixture through cheesecloth, pressing fruit to remove all liquid. Strain again through coffee filters as many times as necessary to produce absolutely clear vinegar.

Thread 8 fresh whole cranberries onto each skewer and insert into bottles. Pour filtered vinegar into bottles to within 2-inches of top. Cap or cork and store in cool dark place.
Yield: 2 (8-ounce) bottles

Cranberry vinegar makes a thoughtful and non-caloric gift, especially when a personalized label is attached. Recipe may be multiplied to suit your gift-giving needs. A little goes a long way!

Although fresh cranberries are in season during the holidays, the editors found this salsa better tasting and less time consuming when made with whole berry cranberry sauce. Native Americans made the first cranberry sauce, sweetening the berries with maple sugar.

CRANBERRY SALSA

1 (16-ounce) can whole cranberry sauce
2 tablespoons finely chopped jalapeño pepper
2 tablespoons chopped sweet onion
2 teaspoons finely grated ginger
1 teaspoon grated orange rind
3 tablespoons fresh orange juice
1 tablespoon red wine vinegar
1 tablespoon tequila
1/2 teaspoon ground cumin, or more if desired
1/4 cup chopped fresh cilantro

Combine all ingredients in medium mixing bowl. Set aside for about 1 hour to allow flavors to blend. Serve with flatbread, toasted mini pitas, or as a condiment for poultry or pork.
Yield: 2 cups

... a make-ahead treat to have on hand when friends drop in for a bit of Christmas cheer.

CRANBERRY CHUTNEY CHEESE BALL

1 (8-ounce) package cream cheese, softened
2 tablespoons sour cream
2 teaspoons curry powder
1/2 cup raisins
1/2 cup dry roasted peanuts, chopped
1/2 cup green onions, minced
1 cup cranberry chutney

Combine cream cheese, sour cream and curry powder in mixer bowl; beat at medium speed until smooth. Stir in raisins, peanuts, and green onions. Shape into ball, cover, and chill at least one hour.

To serve, place cheese ball on serving plate and spoon cranberry chutney over. Serve with crackers or melba toast.
Yield: 8 servings

JEWELED CRANBERRY SALAD

1 (12-ounce) package fresh cranberries, washed and chopped
3/4 cup chopped pecans
1 (8-ounce) can crushed pineapple in own juice, drained
1 (3-ounce) package lemon gelatin
1 teaspoon unflavored gelatin
1 cup granulated sugar
1 cup boiling water

A jewel-colored jellied salad that sparkles when served in a crystal bowl, if you have one. If not, just ask Santa!

Combine cranberries, pecans, and pineapple in small bowl and set aside. In medium saucepan, blend gelatins and sugar together. Add boiling water and stir over low heat until dissolved. Chill gelatin mixture until partially set. Fold in fruit and nut mixture and spoon into pretty 2-quart serving bowl. Chill until set.

Topping
1 (8-ounce) package cream cheese, softened
1/2 cup confectioners' sugar
Pinch salt
1 cup whipping cream
3 tablespoons chopped nuts

Cream cheese, sugar, and pinch of salt together. In separate bowl, whip cream until soft peaks form and fold into cheese mixture. Spoon over chilled salad and sprinkle nuts on top. Chill until serving time.
Yield: 10 servings

CRANBERRY SWEET POTATO BAKE

...perhaps the least complicated really good cranberry side dish you'll ever make.

4 to 6 small sweet potatoes, peeled and cut into rounds
1 (16-ounce) can whole cranberry sauce
1/2 cup orange juice
2 tablespoons brown sugar

Preheat oven to 350 degrees. Arrange sweet potatoes in buttered baking dish. Stir together cranberry sauce, orange juice and brown sugar. Spoon mixture over sweet potatoes. Bake at 350 degrees for one hour covered, and one-half hour uncovered. Bake when something else is being baked, for it reheats well. Or make ahead and reheat.
Yield: 8 servings

CRANBERRY APPLE CRUMBLE

Down home simplicity with a sophisticated taste; especially when served with vanilla-bean ice cream.

2 cups fresh cranberries, washed and picked over
3 to 4 Granny Smith apples, peeled, cored, and sliced
3/4 cup granulated sugar
1 cup rolled oats
1/2 cup brown sugar
1/2 cup chopped pecans
1/2 cup (I stick) butter, melted

Preheat oven to 350 degrees. Toss together apples, cranberries and granulated sugar. Transfer to buttered baking dish. Mix together rolled oats, brown sugar and pecans; spread evenly over apple-cranberry mixture. Pour melted butter evenly over top. Bake at 350 degrees for 40 minutes.
Yield: 8 servings

CRANBERRY PISTACHIO BISCOTTI

8 ounces shelled pistachios
8 tablespoons unsalted butter
1/2 cup granulated sugar
2 eggs
1/2 teaspoon vanilla extract
2 cups all-purpose flour
2 teaspoons baking powder
1/4 teaspoon salt
3/4 cup dried cranberries, coarsely chopped

These sensational twice-baked dipping biscuits studded with dried cranberries, are perfect at any time of day … from morning caffe latte to afternoon cappuccino or with a glass of Vin Santo to end the evening.

Preheat oven to 350 degrees. Grease or spray baking sheet and set aside. Place pistachio nuts in tea towel and rub together vigorously to remove as much skin as possible. Reserve some whole nuts. Coarsely chop remainder and recombine with whole nuts.

In large mixer bowl cream butter, sugar, eggs, and vanilla until light and fluffy. Sift together flour, baking powder and salt. Add pistachios and cranberries. Toss to coat evenly with flour mixture. Gradually stir flour mixture into butter mixture. Turn onto floured board and shape into loaf 3 x 10-inches long. Transfer loaf to baking sheet. Bake 30 minutes, or until lightly browned.

Remove from oven, reduce oven heat to 275 degrees. Cut loaf on-the-diagonal into 1/2-inch slices. Return to oven and toast 15 minutes on each side, or until golden brown. Cool thoroughly before storing in air-tight containers. Will keep up to 2 weeks.
Yield: 18 biscotti

"Keeping" means that the cake improves with age, but some cooks want to keep it all for themselves! It can also be baked very successfully in mini loaf pans for gift giving.

CRANBERRY KEEPING CAKE

2 1/2 cups fresh cranberries
2/3 cup granulated sugar
1 tablespoon water
1 teaspoon grated orange peel
2 1/4 cups all-purpose flour
2 teaspoons ground cinnamon
1/2 teaspoon ground coriander
1/2 teaspoon ground cardamom
1/4 teaspoon ground cloves
3/4 teaspoon salt
2 eggs
2 cups brown sugar
3/4 cup sour cream
2 teaspoons baking soda dissolved in
2 teaspoons water
1/2 cup butter, melted and cooled
2/3 cup coarsely chopped pecans

Preheat oven to 350 degrees. Grease and line with parchment 2 (9 x 5 x 3-inch) loaf pans; set aside. Combine 1 1/2 cups of the cranberries, sugar, water and orange peel and cook over medium heat, stirring frequently, until berries have popped. Remove from heat. Coarsely chop remaining cranberries; add to cooked ones and cool.

Sift together flour, spices, and salt. In large mixer bowl beat eggs, brown sugar, sour cream and soda dissolved in water. Stir in dry ingredients. Blend in butter; fold in cranberries and nuts. Blend until combined. Divide batter between loaf pans. Bake in center of oven 1 hour or until cakes test done. Cool on racks, wrap well and refrigerate at least 3 or 4 days before serving. Cakes age and freeze well.

Yield: 2 large loaf cakes

CRUSTLESS CRANBERRY PIE

2 cups cranberries, washed, picked over, and dried
1/2 cup roughly chopped pecans
1/2 cup granulated sugar
2 eggs
1 cup granulated sugar
1/4 cup shortening, melted
1/2 cup butter, melted
1 cup flour

Preheat oven to 325 degrees. Grease a 9-inch pie plate.
Place cranberries in pie plate. Combine nuts and sugar;
sprinkle over cranberries. Beat eggs with 1 cup sugar,
melted shortening and butter. Add flour and stir
together until well blended. Pour batter over cranberries and bake 1 hour. Best served warm with ice-cream
or whipped cream.
Yield: 8 servings

… an all-American cranberry offering closely related to a French claflouti… ever so down home and delicious.

HOLIDAY CRANBERRY PIE

Pastry for 1 double-crust pie
2 cups fresh cranberries, chopped
1/2 cup raisins, chopped
1 large baking apple, peeled, cored, and chopped
Dash of salt
1 cup granulated sugar (reserve 1 tablespoon for crust)
1 teaspoon vanilla extract
Grated rind of 1 orange
1 tablespoon milk

Preheat oven to 450 degrees. Place one pie crust in
9-inch pie plate. In a bowl toss together cranberries,
raisins, apple, salt, sugar, vanilla and orange rind.
Spoon mixture into unbaked pie crust and cover with
top crust. Seal edges, trim, and cut vent slits. Brush top
crust with milk and sprinkle with granulated sugar.
Bake at 450 degrees for 10 minutes. Reduce
temperature to 350 degrees and continue baking about
45 minutes, or until crust is nicely browned.
Yield: 8 servings

Add seasonal decorations … perhaps pastry stars, holly leaves, or a circle of miniature Christmas trees.

CRANBERRY BAKED ALASKA

A dramatic finale for elegant holiday dinners or a show-stopping dessert for an Island after-theatre dessert party.

2 packages (about 6-dozen) lady fingers
3 quarts vanilla ice cream, slightly softened
1 1/2 cups whole cranberry sauce, chilled
6 tablespoons brandy
1/8 teaspoon each salt and cream of tartar
3 egg whites, at room temperature
3/4 cup granulated sugar

Two or three days before needed, line bottom of 9-inch springform pan completely with lady fingers. Stand lady fingers upright around outer edge, trimming to come just to top of pan. Place softened ice cream in mixing bowl. Add cranberry sauce and brandy; swirl into ice cream. Spoon ice-cream mixture into prepared spring form pan. Cover with plastic wrap and place in freezer.

About 2 hours before needed, beat salt and cream of tartar into egg whites. When frothy, gradually beat in sugar to achieve meringue consistency. Remove dessert from freezer, spread with meringue, sealing edges, and return, uncovered, to freezer.

Preheat oven to 475 degrees just prior to serving. Transfer dessert to oven. Bake 5 minutes or until meringue is lightly browned. Remove sides of springform pan; transfer Baked Alaska to cake plate. Slice into wedges and serve immediately with Brandy Sauce if desired.
Yield: 12 servings

Brandy Sauce
2 teaspoons corn starch
1/4 cup brandy
1 1/2 cups whole cranberry sauce

In sauce pan dissolve cornstarch in brandy. Add cranberry sauce and stir to combine. Cook over moderate heat until thick and glossy. Serve warm from a sauce boat.

SHERRIED CRANBERRY DESSERT SAUCE

1 cup granulated sugar
1 cup dry sherry
2 cups fresh cranberries, washed and picked over
1/2 cup chopped walnuts

Place sugar and sherry in non-reactive saucepan over low heat. Stir until sugar is dissolved. Increase heat and bring to boil. Add cranberries and cook about 8 minutes or until cranberries pop. Cool and stir in walnuts.
Yield: 2 cups

A lovely combination that's great for topping ice creams, meringues, frozen yogurt, or pancakes. Suddenly you have a special occasion dessert.

CRANBERRY ORANGE SAUCE

1 small unpeeled orange, sliced
2 1/3 cups orange juice
2 cups granulated sugar
3 scant tablespoons lemon juice
1 (12-ounce) package fresh cranberries, washed and picked over
3 tablespoons Grand Marnier, or other orange liqueur

Finely grind orange in food processor. Combine orange juice, sugar and lemon juice in heavy gauge non-reactive saucepan. Bring to boil and stir until sugar dissolves. Reduce heat and simmer 5 minutes. Add ground orange and cranberries. Cook about 8 minutes or until cranberries have popped. Cool, cover and refrigerate or freeze.
Yield: 12 servings

The unmistakable flavor of fresh orange and a touch of Grand Marnier makes this holiday sauce so good.

LEA'S CRANBERRY BREAD

A quick and easy cranberry bread to have on hand throughout the holidays. Watch it disappear! Delightful to include on a cheese board.

2 cups cranberries, sliced and set aside
1 cup all-purpose flour
1 cup unprocessed bran
2 teaspoons baking powder
1/2 teaspoon baking soda
1 cup granulated sugar
1 egg, slightly beaten
2 tablespoons melted butter
3/4 cup freshly squeezed orange juice
1 to 2 tablespoons grated orange zest
1 cup chopped pecans (optional)

Preheat oven to 375 degrees. Grease or spray 3 (5 x 3 x 2-inch) loaf pans. Combine flour, bran, baking powder, baking soda, and sugar in large bowl. In separate bowl, mix together beaten egg, melted butter, orange juice and orange zest; add to dry ingredients and stir gently just until moistened. Fold in sliced cranberries and nuts. Divide batter among pans.

Bake 45 to 50 minutes or until top springs back when touched. Cool in pans on rack 10 minutes, then turn out and cool completely. Wrap well and store in cool place. Keeps beautifully.
Yield: 3 loaves

FRESH CRANBERRY CURD

3 1/2 cups fresh cranberries, picked over and washed
1 cup granulated sugar
5 egg yolks
1 tablespoon fresh lemon juice
1/8 teaspoon salt
1/2 cup unsalted butter, melted and boiling hot
2 tablespoons Kirsch or brandy

Cook cranberries and 1/2 cup sugar over low heat until very soft. Transfer to food processor and purée. Force purée through strainer. Return to food processor. Add egg yolks, remaining sugar, lemon juice and salt. Pour hot butter through feed tube while processing.

Return mixture to saucepan; cook to 170 degrees stirring constantly. Cool and refrigerate until needed, up to one month. Stir in Kirsch or brandy just before serving.
Yield: 2 cups

A devine confection for filling tiny tart shells. Top with a wee dab of whipped cream to make it doubly delicious.

Cook's Note:
A candy thermometer, used here, is a very useful tool to have in your kitchen.

CRANBERRY SORBET

2 cups cranberries, washed and picked over
1/4 cup fresh orange juice
1 tablespoon fresh lemon juice
1 tablespoon grated orange zest
3 cups water
1 cup granulated sugar
2 tablespoons orange liqueur

Place berries, juices, zest, and 1/2 cup of water in saucepan. Cook until berries pop. Coarsely mash berries. Add remaining water and sugar. Simmer, stirring often, until a syrup forms. Cool; place in covered container and freeze.

About 2 hours before serving, break up frozen sorbet. Transfer to food processor, add liqueur and process until smooth. Return to freezer until serving time.
Yield: 4 cups

This bright, rose-red sorbet can also be a delightful palate refresher.

VISUAL & PERFORMING ARTS

Simply superb! The cultural climate on Hilton Head Island couldn't be more inviting or interesting. We are endowed with a medley of visual and performing arts – including dance, theater, music, and art.

The 1996 opening of our grandly designed Self Family Arts Center set the stage for an enduring future of artistic endeavors. This ten-million dollar art center offers professional theater productions, art exhibits, art and drama workshops, and performing arts series of unparalleled breadth and variety.

The Hilton Head Playhouse has taken full advantage of the state-of-the-art 360 seat Elizabeth Wallace Theater to produce spectacular musicals, dramas, and comedies. Productions feature elaborate sets, lighting, and sound.

On the visual arts side, the Walter Greer Gallery has presented just as wide a range of arts and culture from the centuries-old pottery of the Catawba Indians to the whimsical work of folk artists. The Hilton Head Art League is gaining recognition as an art mecca. Their annual workshop series attracts artists from across the country.

Quickly becoming the jewel in the crown of our multi-faceted cultural program is the Hilton Head Dance Theater. Their incredible showcase of talent includes presentations of the Nutcracker; The Great Fairy Tale Ballet Series; Terpsichery, the program for gifted and talented dancers; and Prologue, a vibrant outreach program. The First Night Series brings notable dance companies such as New York's Ballet Hispanica. Once the principle dancer in New York's American Ballet Theater, Karena Brock Carlyle, with husband John, are artistic directors.

The sound of music is a year-long season here, with world class musical super stars appearing alongside emerging artists. The Hilton Head Orchestra, under the direction of Mary Woodmansee Green, is one of broad scope and unusual diversity. The Hilton Head Chorale, Hilton Head String Quartet, and Children's Youth Orchestra all show incredible talent.

The thriving Island arts continue to add a vital and permanent element to our community.

page 134

ISLANDERS FAVORITE FINALES

Southerners treasure their sweets ... and

no holiday would be complete without the grande finale.

In this collection you'll find some simple holiday

favorites, with some all-time classics,

and some sinfully decadent creations... all

with a memorable impression.

The editors can vouch for the mmms and aaahs

that will come with each silken bite.

SORBETS IN MERINGUE NESTS
WITH RASBERRY COULIS

8 meringues (recipe follows)
Raspberry coulis (recipe follows)
3 pints sorbet (or sherbet) in raspberry, lemon, and lime flavors
8 sprigs fresh mint

Meringues make festive party fare. They're especially good when complemented with the cool flavors of raspberry, lemon, and lime.

Film bottoms of individual dessert plates with raspberry coulis. Center meringue on plate. Fill center with 1 scoop of each sorbet. Drizzle a little coulis over top and garnish with a sprig of mint.

Meringues
3 egg whites at room temperature
1/4 teaspoon cream of tartar
1/2 cup superfine sugar
1/2 teaspoon vanilla extract

Preheat oven to 200 degrees. Line large baking sheet with parchment. In large mixer bowl beat egg whites with cream of tartar until soft peaks form. Adding sugar gradually, beat whites until stiff and shiny. Beat in vanilla. Drop meringue in 8 mounds onto parchment. With back of spoon make indentation in each mound. Bake 1 hour. Turn off heat, leave oven door closed, and allow to dry overnight. Freeze if not using right away.

Raspberry Coulis
1 (16-ounce) package unsweetened frozen raspberries, thawed
2 tablespoons superfine granulated sugar
1 teaspoon lemon juice
1 to 2 tablespoons orange or raspberry liqueur

Place all ingredients in blender; purée until smooth. Strain to remove seeds.

Yield: 8 desserts

A light and

contemporary Bavarian

reminiscent of

Nesselrode Pudding.

1 (9-ounce) box chocolate wafer cookies, crumbled
2 tablespoons granulated sugar
3 tablespoons melted butter
1 cup glacé fruits and peels, chopped
1/4 cup chopped red glacé cherries
1/4 cup chopped green glacé cherries
1/4 cup dark rum
2 envelopes unflavored gelatin
3 cups milk
6 eggs, separated
2 teaspoons vanilla extract
1/8 teaspoon salt
2/3 cup granulated sugar
Semisweet chocolate shavings for garnish
A few red and green glacé cherries

Combine chocolate crumbs, sugar, and melted butter. Press into bottom of an 8-inch springform pan and up sides an inch or so. Set aside.

Place glacé fruits, peels, and cherries in a bowl and stir in rum. Allow to stand while preparing remainder of recipe.

Soften gelatin in small amount of milk in saucepan; add remainder of milk. Whisk egg yolks until foamy; add to milk. Cook over low heat (or in double boiler) until gelatin has dissolved and mixture coats a spoon (about 5 minutes). Cool. Stir in fruits, vanilla and salt. Chill until mixture begins to set and will mound on spoon.

Meanwhile, over simmering water, beat egg whites until foamy. Continue to beat while slowly adding sugar until firm peaks have formed; fold into gelatin base. Spoon mixture into prepared springform pan. Cover with plastic wrap. Chill several hours. Decorate with chocolate shavings and a few red and green cherries. Yield: 8 servings

EGGNOG CRÈME BRULÉE

2 1/2 cups heavy cream
3/4 cup granulated sugar, divided
1/4 cup firmly packed brown sugar
1 1/2 teaspoons ground nutmeg, divided
5 egg yolks
3 tablespoons brandy
1 tablespoon vanilla extract

The distinct flavor of eggnog highlights this seasonal variation of the classic ... it definitely says 'Christmas'!

Preheat oven to 300 degrees. Butter a 1 1/2-quart baking dish and set aside. Place cream in medium saucepan and bring to boil over medium-high heat. Remove from heat.

In large mixer bowl, combine 1/2 cup of sugar, egg yolks, brandy, vanilla, and 1/2 teaspoon nutmeg. With electric beaters beat until fluffy, scraping down sides of bowl once. Slowly add 1 cup of the hot cream, stirring constantly. When well blended, add remaining hot cream. Pour into prepared baking dish.

Place dish in hot water bath and bake about 1 hour, or until custard is just set around edge. Cool and refrigerate 6 hours.

Preheat broiler. Combine remaining 1/4 cup of sugar, brown sugar, and remaining nutmeg. Sprinkle over chilled custard. Place 6 to 8 inches beneath broiler, watching carefully, until sugars melt and caramelize. Serve immediately.
Yield: 8 servings

FRUIT TRIFLE

1 recipe sponge cake (recipe follows) or one
purchased from bakery
1 recipe custard sauce (recipe follows)
2/3 cup seedless raspberry jam
1/2 cup medium dry sherry
2 pints fresh raspberries (or frozen whole
unsweetened raspberries)
2 kiwi fruit, peeled and sliced
2 large navel oranges, peeled and sectioned
1 to 2 bananas, peeled and sliced 1/2 inch on diagonal
1/2 cup heavy cream stiffly beaten, lightly sweetened
1/4 cups toasted sliced almonds

Split sponge cake into two layers, spread with raspberry
jam and sandwich back together. Cut into 4-inch
fingers. Line sides and bottom of a 2 1/2 quart glass
bowl with fingers and brush surfaces with sherry.
Spoon half of custard onto bottom. Arrange half of
fruits over custard. Top with sponge cake fingers, and
repeat layers of custard and fruit. Make sure last layer of
fruit is covered with custard. Chill covered, at least 3 to
4 hours.

Before serving, pipe a decorative edge of whipped
cream around outer edge. Garnish with toasted
almonds and additional fresh raspberries.

Sponge Cake
1 cup all-purpose flour
1 1/2 tablespoons cornstarch
1 teaspoon baking powder
Pinch salt
4 eggs, separated, at room temperature
3/4 cup, plus 1 tablespoon granulated sugar
4 tablespoons cold water
1 teaspoon vanilla
Few drops almond flavoring (optional)

Preheat oven to 350 degrees. Prepare a 9-inch square pan with baking spray.

Sift together the flour, cornstarch, baking powder and salt. Sift once more, leave in sifter.

In small mixer bowl, beat egg whites until stiff. Set aside. In large mixer bowl, beat egg yolks until very light. Gradually beat in sugar, water and flavorings. Continue beating until light and lemon colored.

Sift dry ingredients directly over yolk mixture, gradually fold in. Next, fold in beaten whites. Spoon batter into prepared pan. Bake about 30 minutes, or until cake begins to pull away from sides of pan. Cool 10 minutes, remove to cooling rack.

Custard Sauce
2 cups whole milk
1/4 cup granulated sugar
1/8 teaspoon salt
3 eggs
1 teaspoon vanilla extract
1 tablespoon Grand Marnier
1 teaspoon grated orange zest
1 cup heavy cream, whipped

Combine milk and sugar in saucepan, heat to scalding. Meanwhile, add salt to eggs and beat well. Whisk hot milk mixture slowly into eggs and return to saucepan. Cook over low heat stirring, about 10 minutes or until mixture coats a metal spoon. Remove from heat. When cool add vanilla, Grand Marnier and orange zest. Refrigerate to chill. Fold whipped cream into sauce before assembling trifle.
Yield: 10 servings

Back in the late sixteenth century when trifle first appeared in England, it was little more than sweetened cream. These days, it has become an impressive layered wonder. This Hilton Head Island version is worthy of any holiday celebration.

PUMPKIN AMARETTO MOUSSE

Search no further for a
refreshing, light,
Thanksgiving dessert; all
the more enjoyable when
accompanied with a sip
or two of Amaretto.

2 tablespoons unflavored gelatin
1/2 cup cold water
1/2 cup Amaretto liqueur
1/2 cup granulated sugar
1 tablespoon lemon juice
1 1/2 teaspoons ground cinnamon
1 teaspoon ground ginger
2 cups canned pumpkin
1 cup sour cream
1 cup heavy cream, whipped
Additional whipped cream for garnish
Chopped walnuts for garnish

Place gelatin in heat-proof glass measuring cup. Stir in cold water to soften gelatin. Place in microwave on high for 45 seconds, or until gelatin has dissolved and turned clear.

Meanwhile, combine Amaretto, sugar, and lemon juice; stir in gelatin and set aside. Combine cinnamon and ginger with pumpkin; fold in sour cream and whipped cream.

Fold gelatin mixture into pumpkin mixture. Spoon into an oiled 6-cup mold; refrigerate until set.

To serve, unmold mousse onto serving plate. Garnish top with whipped cream and chopped walnuts.
Yield: 8 servings

CHRISTMAS PLUM PUDDING
WITH HARD SAUCE

3/4 cup all-purpose flour
1 1/4 cups fresh bread crumbs
6 ounces butter
1 cup raisins
3/4 cup currants
1 cup grated apple
2/3 cup granulated sugar
Scant 1/2 cup chopped candied citrus peel
1/2 teaspoon each ground cinnamon, allspice, nutmeg, and cloves
1/4 cup brandy
Grated peel and juice of 1 orange
3 eggs

Grease 4-cup bowl and line bottom with a circle of waxed paper. Mix ingredients together in order given and spoon into prepared bowl. Tie doubled waxed paper and aluminum foil onto bowl to cover. Place bowl on rack or trivet over simmering water in covered kettle. Steam for 4 hours. Allow to cool. Replace original cover with fresh waxed paper and foil. Store up to a year in cool, dry place. Re-steam for 1 1/2 hours just prior to serving. Serve with Hard Sauce.

Hard Sauce
1 cup unsalted butter, softened
1 cup confectioners' sugar
1/4 cup brandy

In large mixer bowl beat butter at high speed 1 minute, or until creamy. On low speed, beat in sugar, followed by brandy. Prepare up to 2 weeks ahead, cover tightly and refrigerate. Bring to room temperature before serving. Yield: 6 to 8 servings

According to an old English tradition, the number of homes in which you eat Plum Pudding during the 12 days following Christmas will be the number of happy and lucky months you'll have during the coming year.

STEAMED PERSIMMON PUDDING
WITH RUM SAUCE

This surprisingly light pudding came to Hilton Head Island via California. Lucky for us, persimmons grow well in the South and appear to proliferate in Charleston courtyards.

6 tablespoons unsalted butter, melted
3/4 cup granulated sugar
3/4 cup sifted all-purpose flour
1/8 teaspoon salt
3/4 teaspoon Chinese Five Spice powder
1 cup puréed fresh persimmon (very ripe, almost mushy)
1 1/4 teaspoons baking soda, dissolved in 1 1/4 tablespoons hot water
1 1/4 tablespoons brandy
1/4 teaspoon vanilla extract
1/8 cup each raisins and currants
3/4 teaspoon lemon juice
1/4 cup chopped walnuts
2 eggs, lightly beaten

Add sugar to melted butter. Sift together flour, salt and spice powder; stir into butter mixture. Add persimmon, soda, brandy, vanilla, raisins, currants, lemon juice, nuts and eggs. Mix well and pour into 4-cup well-buttered pudding mold with clamp-on cover, or cover 4-cup bowl with doubled wax paper and aluminum foil tied in place. Place pudding mold on rack or trivet over simmering water in covered kettle. Steam for 1 1/4 hours. May be made ahead and refrigerated. Re-steam for about 40 minutes prior to serving. Serve sliced and topped with Rum Sauce.
Yield: 6 to 8 servings

Rum Sauce
1 (3-ounce) package cream cheese, softened
2 tablespoons butter, softened
1 teaspoon lemon juice
Pinch salt
1 cup confectioners' sugar
1 cup heavy cream, whipped
2 tablespoons dark rum

Beat cream cheese until light and fluffy. Continue beating while adding butter, lemon juice, salt and confectioners' sugar. Fold in whipped cream and rum. Refrigerate, covered, until needed.

VIENNESE CHESTNUT TORTE
MIT SCHLAG

1 (15 1/2-ounce) can unsweetened whole chestnuts, drained and patted dry
1 cup granulated sugar
4 eggs, room temperature
1 cup unsalted butter, room temperature
1/4 cup whipping cream
3 tablespoons dark rum
1 tablespoon vanilla extract
1/4 teaspoon salt

Whipped Cream Topping
1 1/2 cups chilled whipping cream
2 tablespoons sugar
1/2 teaspoon vanilla extract
Candied violets for garnish (optional)

This 'perfect ending' dessert is a cross between a thick mousse and penuche candy.

Position rack in center of oven. Preheat to 300 degrees. Line a 5-cup ovenproof bowl with foil; oil lightly.

Purée chestnuts with sugar in food processor. Add eggs, process 1 minute. Add butter, 1/4 cup cream, rum, vanilla and salt. Process about 2 minutes or until smooth. Transfer to prepared bowl.

Bake torte about 1 1/2 hours or until fluffy and light brown. (Center will crack and depress slightly.) Cool completely in bowl. Cover and refrigerate at least 12 hours or up to 3 days.

Unmold torte on serving plate, and remove foil. Whip cream with sugar and vanilla to form stiff peaks. Spoon into pastry bag and cover torte completely with rosettes. Or alternately, frost torte with whipped cream and swirl with metal spatula. Garnish randomly with candied violets.
Yield: 12 servings

CHOCOLATE MOUSSE CAKE

6 eggs, separated
1 1/2 cups granulated sugar, divided
1/2 cup all-purpose flour
1 cup cocoa, divided
1 pint whipping cream
2 tablespoons rum
1/2 cup apricot preserves
1 tablespoon Triple-Sec
8 ounces semi-sweet chocolate
2 1/2 tablespoons canola oil

Preheat oven to 350 degrees. Line a 9-inch metal bowl with well-greased foil. Set aside. Beat 6 egg whites until frothy. Gradually add 1/4 cup of sugar while beating to firm peaks. Set aside. With same beaters beat 6 egg yolks and 3/4 cup of sugar until pale yellow and mixture forms ribbon when beaters are lifted. Fold beaten yolks carefully into beaten whites.

Sift together flour and 1/2 cup of cocoa. Fold into egg mixture. Pour into foil lined bowl; bake 15 minutes. Reduce oven temperature to 325 degrees; continue baking 30 to 35 minutes. Cool in pan on rack 15 minutes. Invert onto rack and cool completely. Peel away foil. Cake will have shrunk. Place on serving plate. Cut a 1-inch lid from top of cake; scoop out inside leaving 1-inch shell. Tear inner pieces into chunks and sprinkle with rum.

…a complex procedure,

with a delicious result.

Combine remaining 1/2 cup of sugar and cocoa. Beat cream to firm peak stage while adding sugar-cocoa mix. Fold rum-soaked pieces into half the cocoa whipped cream; spoon into cake shell. Place lid on top. Whisk apricot preserves and Triple-Sec together, heat to boiling; force through sieve. Brush mixture over surface of cake to glaze. Cool.

Combine semi-sweet chocolate and canola oil. Melt over hot water, whisking until smooth. While still hot, pour over surface of cake to cover completely. Chill until hardened. Place remaining cocoa whipped cream in pastry bag with decorative tip. Decorate top of cake as desired. Refrigerate until needed.

Yield: 12 servings

NANA'S CHOCOLATE CAKE

"Learned at the side of a special grandma during World War II, when rationing was a way of life, this dense and delicious cake survived and lives on today."

1 2/3 cups sifted all-purpose flour
1/3 cup unsweetened Dutch process cocoa
3/4 teaspoon baking powder
1/4 teaspoon baking soda
1/2 teaspoon salt
3/4 cup unsalted butter
1 1/2 cups granulated sugar
3 eggs, lightly beaten
3/4 cup milk

Preheat oven to 325 degrees. Butter two 9-inch round cake pans, dust with cocoa. Set aside. Sift together flour, cocoa, baking powder, soda and salt. Set aside. Cream butter and sugar together. Beat in eggs; beating until pale yellow. To the mixture, alternately add flour mixture and milk, beginning and ending with flour. Continue beating 2 minutes after last addition.

Spoon batter into prepared pans and bake 25 minutes or until cakes test done. Cool cakes 15 minutes before removing from pans. Cool completely on wire racks and spread with Milk Chocolate Frosting (recipe follows).

Milk Chocolate Frosting
1/2 pound unsalted butter, softened
2/3 cup unsweetened Dutch process cocoa
3 cups sifted confectioners' sugar
1/2 cup milk
1 1/2 teaspoons vanilla extract

Cream butter until light; beat in cocoa and confectioners' sugar alternately with milk. Add vanilla. Refrigerate until spreadable. Fill between cake layers; frost sides and top. Refrigerate until needed.
Yield: 12 servings

GRANDMA'S THUNDER CAKE

2 1/2 cups cake flour
1/2 cup cocoa powder
1 1/2 teaspoons baking soda
1 teaspoon salt
1 cup cold water
1/3 cup puréed tomatoes
3 eggs, separated
1 cup vegetable shortening
1 3/4 cups granulated sugar
1 teaspoon vanilla extract
1 pint strawberries, washed and hulled

... and the applause thunders on for Grandma's creamy chocolate cake, topped with temptation and served with fresh strawberries.

Preheat oven to 350 degrees. Spray two 9-inch cake pans and line with parchment; set aside. Sift together cake flour, cocoa, baking soda and salt. Combine cold water and puréed tomatoes; set aside. Beat whites until firm peaks form; set aside. Using same beaters, cream together shortening, sugar, vanilla and egg yolks. To creamed mixture, alternately mix in flour mixture and tomato-water, beginning and ending with flour mixture. Gently fold in beaten whites. Divide batter between prepared cake pans. Bake 30 to 35 minutes or until cakes test done. Remove cakes from pans to wire rack.

Cool completely before spreading with Creamy Chocolate Frosting. Refrigerate after frosting. Before serving, garnish top with strawberries.

Creamy Chocolate Frosting
1/4 cup butter, softened
1/4 cup heavy cream
1 teaspoon vanilla extract
1 (1-pound) box confectioners' sugar
1/3 cup unsweetened cocoa powder
1/8 teaspoon salt

Cream together butter, heavy cream and vanilla. Sift together sugar, cocoa and salt; beat into butter mixture until smooth and spreadable.
Yield: 8 to 12 servings

This excellent cake won second prize at the 1996 Yuletide Recipe Contest. The judges welcomed the well rounded set of holiday flavors: cranberry, nuts, dates, and orange plus a final flourish of sherry in the cream.

DOTTIE DUNBAR'S
ORANGE-CRANBERRY TORTE

2 1/4 cups sifted all-purpose flour
1 cup granulated sugar
1/4 teaspoon salt
1 teaspoon baking powder
1 teaspoon baking soda
1 cup chopped English walnuts
1 cup diced dates
1 cup fresh cranberries
Grated rind of 2 oranges
2 eggs, beaten
1 cup buttermilk
1 cup salad oil
1 cup orange juice
1 cup sugar
Sherry-flavored whipped cream

Preheat oven to 350 degrees. Oil 10-inch tube pan and dust with flour. Set aside. Sift together flour, sugar, salt, baking powder and soda. Stir in nuts, dates, cranberries and orange rind.

Combine eggs, buttermilk, and salad oil. Stir into flour and fruit mixture.

Spoon into prepared pan. Bake 1 hour. Let stand until lukewarm; unmold onto rack set over baking sheet.

Stir orange juice and sugar over moderate heat until sugar is dissolved. Slowly pour over lukewarm torte. Gather any excess syrup that falls underneath, and pour again until all is absorbed.

Refrigerate 24 hours before slicing or storing. Store wrapped in foil. Will keep two weeks. Freezes well.

To serve with sherry-flavored whipped cream, beat one cup of whipping cream together with 2 tablespoons each, confectioners' sugar and good Spanish sherry.
Yield: 12 servings

PUMPKIN CAKE
WITH CREAM CHEESE FROSTING

2 cups all-purpose flour
1/2 teaspoon salt
2 teaspoons baking soda
1/2 teaspoon ground ginger
1/4 teaspoon ground nutmeg
1 teaspoon ground cloves
1 teaspoon cinnamon
4 eggs, at room temperature
2 cups granulated sugar
1 cup canola oil
1 (15-ounce) can pumpkin
1/2 cup chopped walnuts
Garnish: tiny pumpkin candies and walnut halves

Children are delighted when candy pumpkins appear on this spicy Thanksgiving Bundt cake.

Preheat oven to 350 degrees. Spray 9-inch Bundt pan with baker's spray. Set aside. Sift together flour, salt, baking soda and spices. Set aside. With electric beaters, cream together eggs and sugar. Continue beating while adding oil and pumpkin. At lower speed, blend flour mixture into pumpkin mixture and fold in chopped walnuts. Spoon batter into prepared pan.

Bake 50 minutes, or until a toothpick inserted into cake comes out clean. Cool in pan on rack for 40 minutes before unmolding onto serving plate. When cool spread with Cream Cheese Frosting (page 153). Garnish top with tiny pumpkin candies and walnut halves.

Yield: 12 servings

RED VELVET CAKE
WITH FLUFFY COCONUT FROSTING

Originally from rural America, this celebration cake was elevated to lofty status on menus at both the Waldorf Astoria and Neiman Marcus. It's now enjoying a new wave of appreciation.

1/2 cup shortening
1 1/2 cups granulated sugar
2 eggs
2 teaspoons cocoa
1 (1-ounce) bottle red food coloring
2 1/2 cups sifted cake flour
1 teaspoon salt
1 cup buttermilk
1 teaspoon vanilla extract
1 teaspoon each vinegar and baking soda

Preheat oven to 350 degrees. Grease or spray 2 (8-inch) round cake pans. Set aside. In large mixer bowl, cream together, shortening and sugar. Beat in eggs, one at a time. Mix cocoa and food coloring to a paste; beat into egg mixture. Add salt to flour; beat into egg mixture alternately with buttermilk. Add vanilla. Combine vinegar and soda; fold into batter (do not beat). Spoon batter into prepared cake pans; bake 25 minutes, or until cake layers test done. Cool on rack. Fill and frost cake with Fluffy Coconut Frosting.
Yield: 12 servings

Fluffy Coconut Frosting
1 cup granulated sugar
1/4 cup water
1/4 teaspoon cream of tartar
Pinch salt
3 large egg whites
1 teaspoon vanilla extract
1/4 teaspoon coconut extract
2/3 cup flaked sweetened coconut

With hand-held mixer at high speed, beat first 5 ingredients in top of double boiler over simmering water, about 7 minutes, to form stiff peaks. Beat in vanilla and coconut extract. After frosting cake, top with flaked coconut.

POOR MAN'S
CINNAMON CAKE

2 cups granulated sugar
3 teaspoons ground cinnamon
1/2 teaspoon salt
1 pound dark raisins
1 cup chopped nuts
3 tablespoons vegetable shortening (or corn oil)
2 cups hot water
3 cups all-purpose flour
1 1/2 teaspoon baking soda

Full of surprises, this cake is low in fat, has no eggs, and a unique method of preparation. It is dense and moist, slices easily, keeps well, and lends itself to any number of frostings.

Preheat oven to 350 degrees. Spray a 9-inch Bundt pan with baker's spray; set aside. Combine first seven ingredients in saucepan; bring to boil and simmer gently for 5 minutes. Remove from heat. Sift together flour and soda and stir into liquid ingredients. Spoon into prepared pan. Bake 55 to 60 minutes or until cake tests done; cool in pan. Spread top and sides with Cream Cheese Frosting (recipe follows). Yield: 16 servings

Cream Cheese Frosting
1 (3-ounce) package cream cheese, softened
2 teaspoons milk
1 teaspoon vanilla extract
Dash salt
1 1/2 cups confectioners' sugar

Mix together cream cheese, milk, vanilla and salt; beat in confectioners' sugar. Continue beating until spreading consistency is reached.

ORANGE SLICE CAKE

One can imagine the fun Aunt Violet had tucking orange candies into the center of this cake.

3 1/2 cups all-purpose flour
1 teaspoon baking soda
1/4 teaspoon salt
1 cup butter
2 cups granulated sugar
4 eggs, beaten until frothy
1 teaspoon vanilla extract
1 cup buttermilk
3 cups coconut
2 cups chopped pecans (or walnuts)
24 jellied orange slice candies, lightly floured

Preheat oven to 325 degrees. Butter an 8-cup tube pan or Bundt pan. Sift together flour, baking soda and salt; set aside. Cream butter and sugar until fluffy. Gradually beat eggs and vanilla into butter and sugar mixture; continue beating until light and pale yellow. Alternately, beat in flour mixture with buttermilk, beginning and ending with flour. Fold in coconut and pecans.

Pour one-third of the cake batter into prepared pan. Layer one half of the candies on batter. Add second layer of batter and candies, and end with batter on top. Bake for 1 hour and 45 minutes. Remove from pan, cool slightly; wrap with foil while still warm. Keep in refrigerator.
Yield: 10 to 12 servings

KENTUCKY BOURBON FRUITCAKE

1 pound raisins
1 pound glacé cherries
2 cups bourbon
3/4 pound butter
1 cup brown sugar
2 cups granulated sugar
6 eggs, separated, at room temperature
3 1/2 cups all-purpose flour
1/4 teaspoon salt
1 teaspoon baking powder
2 teaspoons ground nutmeg
1 pound pecans, tossed with 1/2 cup flour

Most Southerners associate fruitcake with the flavor of bourbon rather than brandy because it all started in Bourbon County, Kentucky.

Marinate cherries and raisins overnight in bourbon.

Next day, preheat oven to 275 degrees. Butter and flour, or spray with baker's spray, 10-inch tube pan. Cream butter, brown sugar and granulated sugar until fluffy; add egg yolks and beat well. Stir in marinated fruits and bourbon. Sift flour, salt, baking powder and nutmeg together; stir into creamed fruit mixture until well-incorporated.

Beat egg whites until firm peaks have formed; fold into creamed mixture. Fold in floured pecans. Pour batter into prepared pan. Bake 3 to 4 hours, or until toothpick inserted into cake comes out clean. Wrap in bourbon-soaked cheesecloth and store in tightly covered container. Make up to one month ahead. Yield: 1 (10-inch) round fruit cake

WHITE CHOCOLATE FRUITCAKE

Even if you're not a fan

of the standard

fruitcakes that come in

those decorated tins,

you'll love this

sophisticated one

chock-full of

bourbon-soaked

dried fruit.

1 cup finely-diced figs
3/4 cup finely-diced dried apples
3/4 cup finely-diced dried apricots
3/4 cup bourbon
1/2 cup finely-diced dried pears
1/2 cup dried currants
1/2 cup chopped dried bananas
1/2 cup unsalted butter, room temperature
1/2 cup plus 1 tablespoon firmly packed golden brown sugar
1 teaspoon vanilla extract
1/2 teaspoon cinnamon
1/4 teaspoon ground cloves
1/4 teaspoon freshly ground nutmeg
4 eggs, separated, room temperature
8 ounces imported white chocolate, melted, lukewarm
1 cup sifted all-purpose flour
1 1/4 cups salted toasted pecans
3 tablespoons all-purpose flour
2 ounces white chocolate, melted

Mix first 7 ingredients in small bowl. Cover and let stand at least 24 hours at room temperature, stirring once.

Preheat oven to 300 degrees. Butter 9 x 5 x 3-inch loaf pan. Line bottom with waxed paper. Dust pan with flour. In large bowl of electric mixer, cream butter with sugar, until light and fluffy. Add vanilla, cinnamon, cloves and nutmeg. Add egg yolks 1 at a time, beating well after each addition. Stir 8-ounces of chocolate and flour into dried fruit mixture. Stir into batter. Using clean dry beaters, beat whites in medium bowl until soft peaks form. Mix 1/3 of whites into batter to lighten, then fold in remaining whites.

Pour batter into prepared pan. Cover with buttered aluminum foil. Place pan in baking dish.

Add enough hot water to dish to come halfway up sides of loaf pan. Bake until toothpick, inserted in center of cake, comes out clean, about 2 1/2 hours. Remove pan from water, cool cake completely on rack. Unmold. Wrap in plastic, then foil. Let stand at least 8 days at room temperature, to allow flavor to mellow.

Dip fork into 2-ounces melted white chocolate. Drizzle decoratively over top of cake. Chocolate can also be piped through plastic bag with corner tip snipped off. Let stand until cool. Cut into slices.

Yield: 10 servings

MALLOW DATE-NUT ROLL

1 pound marshmallows, chopped (do not use miniatures)
1 pound graham crackers, crumbed
1 pound sugared, chopped dates
1 pint half and half
Whipped cream to garnish

Place marshmallows that have been snipped with wet scissors, graham cracker crumbs, dates and walnuts in mixing bowl. Add half and half and stir together until well combined. Mold mixture into 2 x 8-inch cylinder. Roll snugly in plastic wrap; refrigerate. To serve, cut into 1-inch slices. Place on dessert plate and top with dollop of whipped cream.

Yield: 8 servings

A 92-year young Islander says this has been one of her favorite holiday desserts for as long as she can remember. It's great to do ahead and travels well. This roll was always tucked into her daughter's 'return laundry case' at holiday time throughout her college years.

AUNT EMMA'S
RAISIN & PECAN LAYER CAKE
WITH LEMON-COCONUT FROSTING

There's no resisting the taste of this Southern favorite, and frequent main attraction on holiday tables.

Pecan Cake Layers

8 egg whites
2 cups granulated sugar
3 cups all-purpose flour
1 tablespoon baking powder
1 teaspoon vanilla extract
1 cup milk
1 cup pecans, coarsely chopped

Preheat oven to 350 degrees. Butter and flour 4 (9-inch) layer cake pans. Set aside. Beat egg whites until firm peaks have formed. Sift together sugar, flour and baking powder. Add vanilla to milk and blend into flour mixture. Fold in beaten egg whites followed by pecans. Distribute cake batter evenly among prepared cake pans. Bake 20 to 25 minutes, or until cakes test done. Cool on wire rack before removing from pans.

Raisin Cake Layers

2 cups granulated sugar
1 cup vegetable shortening
8 egg yolks
3 cups all-purpose flour
1 tablespoon baking powder
1 teaspoon each ground cloves, cinnamon, ginger, and nutmeg
1 cup milk
2 cups raisins, chopped

Preheat oven to 350 degrees. Butter and flour 4 (9-inch) layer cake pans. Set aside.

Cream together sugar, shortening and egg yolks. Sift together flour and spices. Alternately, blend flour mixture and milk into egg yolk base. When well blended, fold in raisins. Bake 20 to 25 minutes or until cakes test done. Cool pans on wire rack.

When completely cool, fill alternating pecan and raisin layers then frost top and sides with Lemon Coconut Frosting.
Yield: Each cake serves 12

Lemon Coconut Frosting
3 cups granulated sugar
3/4 cup water
Juice of 2 lemons
8 egg whites
8-ounces grated coconut

In saucepan combine sugar, water and lemon juice; cook to soft ball stage (238 degrees). With electric beaters, beat egg whites until stiff but not dry. Continue beating at moderate speed, about 7 minutes, while slowly adding sugar syrup to whites. When light and fluffy, fold in coconut.

Cook's Note:
This recipe creates 2 cakes, each 4 layers high. Recipe may easily be cut in half if only one cake is preferred.

CHEESECAKE
WITH CRANBERRY ORANGE COMPOTE

The freshness of the oranges and the tang of the berries make this cheesecake deliciously different.

1 cup zwieback crumbs
2 tablespoons sugar
1/2 teaspoon cinnamon
3 tablespoons melted butter
3 (8-ounce) packages cream cheese, softened
1/2 teaspoon salt
3 tablespoons orange-flavored liqueur
4 eggs, separated
Pinch of salt
1/4 teaspoon cream of tartar
1 cup granulated sugar
1 1/2 cups dairy sour cream
2 tablespoons sugar

Preheat oven to 350 degrees. Combine zwieback crumbs, sugar, cinnamon and melted butter. Press into bottom of an 8-inch springform pan. Set aside.

Place cream cheese in large mixer bowl; add salt, liqueur, and egg yolks. Beat until well-combined.

Add pinch of salt and cream of tartar to egg whites; with clean beaters, beat until frothy. Gradually add granulated sugar while beating until firm, glossy peaks have formed. Fold into cheese mixture. Turn mixture into prepared crust in springform pan.

Bake 55 minutes. Remove from oven and increase oven temperature to 450 degrees. Add 2 tablespoons sugar to sour cream and spread over cheese cake. Return cake to oven for 5 minutes or until sour cream is set. Remove from oven; cool completely and refrigerate until needed. At serving time, top with Cranberry Orange Compote.
Yield: 10 to 12 servings

Cranberry Orange Compote

1 cup granulated sugar
1/2 cup water
1 (16-ounce) can whole cranberry sauce
2 teaspoons grated orange peel
4 large navel oranges, peeled and sectioned

Combine sugar and water in saucepan; bring to boil stirring until sugar has dissolved. Remove from heat and stir in cranberry sauce and orange peel.

Just prior to serving, add orange sections and stir gently to combine.

DANISH BERRY PUDDING

2 (10-ounce) packages frozen, sweetened sliced strawberries, thawed
2 (10-ounce) packages frozen sweetened raspberries, thawed
1/2 cup cold water
2 tablespoons granulated sugar, plus a little more for finish
1/4 cup cornstarch
Sweetened whipped cream for garnish

Very easy,

very pretty,

and very tasty!

Traditionally served

on Christmas Eve

before church.

Thoroughly drain berries (reserving juices) and place in serving bowl, or in individual dessert dishes. In 1/2 cup cold water in sauce pan, dissolve sugar and cornstarch. Add reserved berry juices. Cook over moderate heat, stirring constantly, until juices have thickened and become translucent, but never allowed to boil. Pour over berries and stir. Sprinkle surface lightly with granulated sugar. Refrigerate until well chilled. Serve with whipped cream.
Yield: 8 servings

OKATIE SWEET POTATO CHEESECAKE

Deliciously rich, this creamy cheesecake is the ultimate splurge of sweet potatoes and spices for the 'y'all' crowd.

Crust
1 1/4 cups graham cracker crumbs
1/4 cup granulated sugar
1/4 cup unsalted butter, melted

Filling
2 pounds sweet potatoes
3 (8-ounce) packages cream cheese, softened
3/4 cup plus 2 tablespoons granulated sugar
1/3 cup sour cream
1/4 cup whipping cream
3 eggs, room temperature

Topping
3/4 cup firmly-packed golden brown sugar
1/4 cup unsalted butter
1/4 cup whipping cream
1 cup chopped toasted pecans

For crust, position rack in center of oven; preheat to 350 degrees. Mix all ingredients. Press mixture into bottom of 9 1/2-inch springform pan. Bake 10 minutes. Cool crust on wire rack. Maintain oven temperature.

For filling, bake sweet potatoes 1 hour or until tender. Remove from oven; cool slightly. Peel potatoes and purée in food processor. Measure 1 1/2 cups purée into large mixer bowl (reserve any remaining for another use). Add cream cheese, sugar, sour cream and cream. Beat until smooth. Add eggs one at a time. Pour filling into crust. Bake 1 hour, or until tests done. Turn off oven; leave cheesecake 1 hour with door ajar.

For topping, heat brown sugar and butter, stirring until sugar dissolves. Increase heat, bring to boil, and stir in cream followed by nuts. Pour mixture, while hot, over cheesecake. Refrigerate at least 8 hours.

Yield: 8 to 10 servings

LIL'S ALMOND STREUSEL APPLE PIE

1 unbaked pie crust
6 to 8 large apples, peeled, cored, and sliced—suggest mixing Granny Smith, Macintosh, and Golden Delicious
2 tablespoons all-purpose flour
1 cup granulated sugar
1 heaping teaspoon ground cinnamon
1/2 cup raisins

The blue ribbon winner of Shelter Cove Oktoberfest in 1990.

Pre-heat oven to 425 degrees. Place pie crust in 9-inch pie plate. Toss together apples, flour, sugar, cinnamon and raisins. Heap into pie crust, arranging carefully to avoid air pockets. Cover apples completely with Streusel Topping. Bake at 425 degrees for 15 minutes, reduce heat to 350 degrees and continue baking 35 minutes.

Basic Pie Crust

1 1/4 cups all-purpose flour
1/4 teaspoon salt
2 tablespoons butter
1/3 cup shortening
3 to 4 tablespoons ice water

Sift and measure flour and salt. Add butter and shortening; cut into flour until fat particles are the size of small peas. Sprinkle ice-water over mixture, and blend with fork, until dough begins to hold together. Shape dough into ball, flatten, wrap, and refrigerate at least 30 minutes before rolling out on floured board.
Yield: 8 servings

Streusel Topping

1/4 cup all-purpose flour
1/2 cup granulated sugar
2 teaspoons ground cinnamon
4 tablespoons butter, cubed
1/2 cup sliced almonds

Cut butter into dry ingredients until broken into small bits, fold in almonds.

Before recorded history, pecan trees grew wild in the South ... lucky for us, they still flourish here. Our largest pecan grove is at the entrance to Moss Creek Plantation where Islanders are often seen filling their hats with these paper-shelled delicacies.

MOSS CREEK PECAN PIE
WITH BOURBON CREAM

1 (9-inch) unbaked pie crust
2 1/2 tablespoons granulated sugar
4 tablespoons all-purpose flour
1 cup light corn syrup
1 cup dark corn syrup
5 eggs, beaten together
1 teaspoon salt
1 1/2 teaspoons vanilla extract
3 tablespoons melted butter
Pecan halves

Preheat oven to 350 degrees. In large mixer bowl, beat together sugar, flour and corn syrup. Beat in eggs, salt, vanilla, and butter. When well-mixed, pour into unbaked pie crust. Decorate top with pecan halves. Bake 45 minutes or until filling is set. Serve with Bourbon Cream.

Cook's Note: To create a version of Derby Pie, scatter 1 cup chocolate chips over bottom of pie crust before pouring in filling.

Bourbon Cream
1/2 cup butter, cubed
1 cup light brown sugar
1/2 cup heavy cream
1/4 cup bourbon

In saucepan whisk butter and sugar constantly over medium heat until sugar has dissolved. Off heat, whisk in cream and then bourbon. Serve warm. May be refrigerated for up to a week and reheated over very low heat.

Yield: 8 slices of pie with 1/4 cup sauce for each

SPICED PUMPKIN FLAN

4 eggs
1 cup sugar, divided
1/4 teaspoon salt
1 teaspoon vanilla
2 teaspoons pumpkin pie spice
1 (15-ounce) can pumpkin
1 2/3 cups evaporated milk

A light, refreshing flan with the flavor of Thanksgiving… and all the flair of an up-to-the-minute dessert terrine. A little whipped cream would be permissible.

Place 1/2 cup sugar in cast iron skillet. Stir with wooden spoon over moderate heat until sugar melts and turns golden. Pour into 9 x 5 x 3-inch loaf pan, tilt to coat bottom and sides as much as possible. Set aside.

Preheat oven to 350 degrees. Beat together eggs, 1/2 cup sugar, salt, vanilla and spice mix. Add to pumpkin and stir to combine. Add evaporated milk and stir until well blended. Pour into prepared loaf pan.

Bake in hot water bath for 1 1/2 hours or until knife blade inserted into center of flan can be withdrawn clean. Cool and refrigerate until serving time.

To serve, run blade of knife between flan and sides of pan. Invert onto serving plate. Add a little water to loaf pan and return to 200-degree oven to further dissolve the caramel. Spoon a little caramel over each slice of flan.

Yield: 8 to 10 servings

AN ISLAND OF GREEN

Beloved Island character Katie Callahan once wrote in her Island Packet Christmas column about living on this lush island that enjoys "The Glory of Green."

The term was first used in Germany to describe the splendor of the Christmas tree introduced by Martin Luther in the 1500's. It happened walking home on Christmas eve when the sight of stars glistening through a Fir tree reminded him of the shining night when Christ was born. He cut down the little tree and took it inside and lit it with candles so that it gleamed as had the one in the woods.

When Captain William Hilton sailed into Port Royal Sound in 1663, our own glorious green was first described. "The headlands is bluff and seems so steep as though trees hung over the water. The lands are laden with tall trees ... oaks, walnuts, and bays, except facing the sea is mostly pines, tall and good."

Well over 300 years later we still enjoy our spreading, sprawling oak trees, dripping with Spanish Moss and perpetually green... the lumps of Mistletoe dangling from tree limbs... the small green Christmas Ferns that grow in the woods.

Islanders observe the birds that swoop down to pick berries from the Cabbage Palmettos. Mocking Birds, Cardinals, Woodpeckers, Bluejays, and Cedar Waxwings berry hunt on native Holly trees. We delight in the Night Herons, Snowy Egrets, King Rails and Woodcocks. Spotting the first Painted Blue Bunting is a ritual each spring – as is the return of Ospreys to their same nests by the bridge that joins us to the mainland.

As the Atlantic ocean spills onto our sandy beaches we enjoy the scurrying Sandpipers, Terns, Gulls, and Yellowlegs. We go shelling and look for a Whelk or a tiny Angel Wing. We look at, but never take live Sand Dollars.

And at night we listen to Green Tree Frogs calling.

$\mathscr{Y}$ULETIDE MORNINGS

Planning breakfasts and brunches during

Yuletide can be a joyous challenge,

as specialties from the old country, from childhood, from

our memory banks of the past,

come to mind and

set us scrambling through clip files

to find just the right recipe.

Look no further,

here you'll find many good recipes suitable

for holiday mornings ...

these, more than any others,

show the international flavor of our Island.

Happily, they'll cast their spell for

many Yuletides to come.

CROISSANT À L'ORANGE

8 small croissants
1 (18-ounce) jar orange marmalade
6 tablespoons orange juice
5 eggs
1 cup heavy cream, or half and half
1 teaspoon almond extract
2 teaspoons grated orange rind
4 orange slices
8 strawberries for garnish
Whipped cream or crème frâiche

Croissants become brunch when baked this way ... an elegant do-ahead for special mornings.

Butter 8 individual oven proof dishes or one 9 x 13-inch baking dish. Split croissants and place bottom halves in dishes. Thin marmalade with orange juice and spread over each bottom half (reserve some for topping glaze). Replace top halves of croissants.

Beat together eggs, heavy cream, almond extract and orange rind. Pour mixture over croissants. Spoon reserved marmalade over tops. Refrigerate overnight.

Preheat oven to 350 degrees. Bake croissants for about 25 minutes. Remove from oven and cool 5 minutes before serving. Garnish each croissant with half slice of orange, a tablespoon of whipped cream and a strawberry.
Yield: 8 servings

COUNTRY HAM, SHIITAKE, AND LEEK STRATA

These creamy eggs have a rich flavor and soufflé-like texture ... perfect for all those friends you've been meaning to invite over to share the holiday spirit. Your 'toast' should be Champagne!

6 tablespoons unsalted butter
5 cups julienned leeks
1/2 pound fresh shiitake mushrooms, stemmed, and cut into 1/4-inch strips
1/2 pound country ham, thinly sliced and cut into 1/4-inch strips
5 cups whipping cream
12 eggs
1 teaspoon freshly grated nutmeg
1 teaspoon salt
Freshly ground black pepper
1 1/2 cups freshly grated Gruyère cheese
Minced fresh parsley, for garnish

Using 1 tablespoon butter for each, butter two 9 x 13-inch shallow baking dishes. Melt remaining butter in heavy large skillet over medium heat. Add leeks and sauté about 8 minutes, until softened. Add mushrooms and sauté 5 minutes. Add ham and sauté 2 minutes. Spread half of mixture over bottom of each dish. You may cover and refrigerate overnight at this point.

Next morning, preheat oven to 375 degrees. Whisk together cream, eggs, nutmeg, salt and pepper. Stir in 1 cup of cheese and pour over ham mixture. Stir contents of baking dishes until ingredients are combined. Top with remaining 1/2 cup cheese. Bake about 30 minutes, or until knife inserted in centers comes out clean and tops are golden brown. Cool 10 minutes. Sprinkle with minced parsley and serve.
Yield: 16 to 18 servings

OVERNIGHT
EGGS PORTUGUESE
WITH SAUSAGE

8 thick slices French bread, cut into 3/4-inch cubes
2 cups grated Cheddar cheese
1 pound lightly-spiced bulk pork sausage
or for more authentic flavor, use Portuguese Linguica
1 (7-ounce) can sliced mushrooms, drained
6 eggs
3 cups milk
1/2 teaspoon salt
1/4 teaspoon freshly ground pepper
3/4 tablespoon prepared mustard
1/3 cup dry vermouth

Lovers of this dish make it on Christmas Eve, and bake it on Christmas morning while gifts are being opened.

Place bread cubes in a greased 9 x 13-inch baking dish. Sprinkle with grated cheese. Brown sausage, breaking it up, and when all fat has been rendered, drain and let cool. Lay over bread and cheese. Top with drained mushrooms. Beat eggs and milk together; add salt, pepper, mustard and vermouth. Pour over mixture in baking dish. Stir gently to combine. Cover and refrigerate overnight.

Next morning, remove from refrigerator 30 minutes before baking. Preheat oven to 350 degrees. Bake 45 to 50 minutes uncovered, or until set. If browning too quickly, tent lightly with foil. Let stand 5 minutes before cutting into large squares to serve.
Yield: 8 servings

Cook's Note: For an interesting variation, chopped onions or red and green pepper could be sautéed in a little olive oil and added along with the mushrooms. Fresh sautéed mushrooms could also be substituted for canned.

BEAUFORT BREAD PUDDING
WITH BERRY SAUCE

2 eggs, lightly beaten
3/4 cup sugar
3 cups milk
1 cup whipping cream or half and half
1/2 cup unsalted butter, melted
1 tablespoon vanilla extract
3/4 cup currants or raisins
1 teaspoon freshly grated nutmeg
8 ounces day-old French bread
Powdered sugar for dusting

In a large bowl, combine eggs, sugar, milk, cream, melted butter, vanilla, currants and nutmeg. Whisk to blend well. Slice bread 1/2-inch thick and place in another bowl.Pour egg mixture over bread. Let stand about 30 minutes, turning frequently, until bread is saturated.

Butter 3-quart baking dish lightly and add the bread slices in layers. Pour any unabsorbed egg mixture over bread. (At this point, pudding can be covered and refrigerated overnight.)

Bake, uncovered, at 350 degrees about 45 minutes, or until custard is set and top is lightly browned. Dust top with powdered sugar. Serve with Berry Sauce.
Yield: 8 servings

Berry Sauce
2 cups fresh or frozen raspberries
2 cups fresh or frozen strawberries
1/3 cup sugar
1/3 cup freshly squeezed orange juice
3 tablespoons freshly squeezed lemon juice

In saucepan, combine all ingredients and simmer about 5 minutes over medium heat. Stir constantly until fruit begins to break up. Transfer to food processor or blender and purée. Reheat just before serving. Makes 2 cups.

LEMON RICOTTA
SOUFFLÉ PANCAKES

6 eggs, separated
2 cups ricotta cheese
1/4 cup vegetable oil
1 cup all-purpose flour
3 tablespoons granulated sugar
4 teaspoons baking powder
1/2 teaspoon salt
4 teaspoons freshly squeezed lemon juice
1 tablespoon finely grated lemon zest
Fresh raspberries and mint for garnish

On Christmas morning before adults and children scatter to try out new toys, tempt them with these lighter-than-air pancakes.

Preheat griddle or skillet. Preheat oven to 250 degrees. In large bowl, beat egg whites until stiff but not dry. In another bowl, combine egg yolks and remaining ingredients (except garnish). Pour into bowl of blender or food processor and blend until smooth. Return to bowl and fold in beaten whites.

Brush griddle with oil. Spoon about 3 tablespoons of batter onto griddle to make silver dollar size pancakes. Flip each over when it becomes bubbly on one side and cook a few minutes longer. Until all are cooked, keep them warm in oven. Serve with Raspberry Sauce garnished with sprig of mint and several fresh raspberries.

Raspberry Sauce
1 pint fresh or 1 (12-ounce) package
unsweetened frozen raspberries
2/3 cup water
1 slice lemon
2/3 cup granulated sugar

Simmer ingredients over moderate heat until sugar has dissolved. Boil rapidly for about 10 minutes, stirring often until mixture has syrupy consistency. Strain and keep warm.
Yield: 6 servings

CHRISTMAS MORNING CINNAMON TOAST

A cross between coffee cake and toast. One bite and you'll have the kids' attention long enough to eat breakfast on Christmas morning.

2 cups all-purpose flour
1 cup granulated sugar
2 teaspoons baking powder
1 teaspoon salt
1 cup milk
2 tablespoons melted butter
1 teaspoon vanilla extract
1/2 cup raisins
1/2 cup melted butter
1/2 cup granulated sugar
1 1/2 teaspoons cinnamon
1/4 teaspoon nutmeg

Preheat oven to 350 degrees. Grease and lightly flour a 15 x 10 x 1-inch jelly roll pan; set aside. Sift together flour, sugar, baking powder, and salt. Blend in milk, melted butter, vanilla and raisins. Mix well and spread in prepared pan. Bake 20 minutes or until golden brown. Drizzle melted butter over hot cake. Combine sugar, cinnamon and nutmeg; sprinkle over top. Return to oven for 10 minutes. Cool slightly before cutting.
Yield: 16 servings

RICH KÜCHEN BRAID

1/4 cup milk
1 package active dry yeast
2 teaspoons granulated sugar
2 eggs, lightly beaten
1 cup evaporated milk or sour cream
4 cups all-purpose flour
3 tablespoons granulated sugar
1 teaspoon salt
1 cup butter, cubed

Icing
1 (1-pound) box confectioners' sugar
1/4 cup evaporated milk (possibly a little more)
1 teaspoon vanilla extract
1/4 cup chopped nuts
12 Maraschino cherries, drained and quartered

"We often make our braids ahead and freeze them. Thawed at room temperature and served with home-frozen peaches, this has become one of our traditional Yuletide breakfasts."

Scald milk; cool to lukewarm. Add yeast and 2 teaspoons sugar; set aside. Meanwhile, beat together eggs and evaporated milk or sour cream; set aside. Sift together flour, sugar and salt. With pastry blender or two knives, cut butter into mixture until evenly distributed.

Combine yeast and egg mixtures, stir into flour until dough is formed. Cover, chill 2 hours, or overnight.

Divide dough into 6 pieces. With floured hands form each piece into a 'rope' and braid 3 'ropes' together. Place braids on lightly greased cookie sheets. Let rise, draft-free, about 1 1/2 hours or until doubled.

Preheat oven to 350 degrees. Bake küchen about 20 minutes or until golden brown.

Beat confectioners' sugar, evaporated milk and vanilla to consistency of heavy cream. Drizzle over tops of braids. Before icing hardens, scatter chopped nuts and cherries over tops. Braids may be made ahead and frozen.

Yield: 12 servings

Cook's Note:
Always handle dough gently when dividing into pieces and braiding.

CHRISTMAS STOLLEN

3 1/2 cups milk, scalded and cooled
2 packages instant dry yeast
1/2 cup lukewarm water
10 cups all-purpose flour, divided
1/2 teaspoon salt
1 1/2 cups butter, at room temperature
2 teaspoons grated lemon rind
5 egg yolks, lightly beaten
1/4 cup brandy
1 pound raisins
1 pound each citron and pecans, chopped
1/2 pound pitted dates, chopped
1/4 pound each red and green glacé cherries, chopped
2/3 cup butter, melted
Confectioners' sugar

Soften yeast in lukewarm water and stir into milk. Stir in 6 cups flour and salt to make soft batter. Place in large oiled bowl. Cover; let rise draft-free until doubled in bulk. Punch down batter; mix in butter, lemon rind, egg yolks and brandy. Work remaining flour in gradually, until dough loosens from bowl. Combine fruits and knead into batter.

Dough will be sticky; divide in half. Place one half at a time on floured surface and roll to 1-inch thickness. Fold one side over to within 1/2-inch of other; seal edges well.   Place each on parchment lined cookie sheet. Let rise until doubled in bulk.

Preheat oven to 350 degrees. Bake stollens 1 hour or until they sound hollow when tapped. Remove sheets to cooling racks. While still warm, drizzle 1/3 cup melted butter over each and sprinkle with confectioners' sugar. When cool, wrap and store.

Yield: 2 traditional stollens

MORAVIAN SUGAR CAKE

1 package active dry yeast
2 teaspoons brown sugar
2 tablespoons warm water
2 medium-small potatoes, peeled and quartered
6 tablespoons butter
6 tablespoons brown sugar
1/2 teaspoon salt
1 egg, lightly beaten
3 cups all-purpose flour
3/4 cup milk at room temperature

Topping
1 cup light brown sugar
1/2 cup butter
1/2 teaspoon cinnamon

Grease or spray 10 x 16-inch baking pan. Dissolve yeast and brown sugar in warm water; set aside.

Boil potatoes 20 minutes, or until tender. Drain and mash. To potatoes add butter and brown sugar; mix well. Transfer ingredients to very large bowl. Stir in beaten egg, 1 cup flour and yeast mixture. Mix in remaining flour alternately with milk until well combined. Place in greased bowl in draft-free area, let rise 1 hour or until doubled in bulk.

Punch dough down and with buttered hands spread evenly in prepared pan. Let rise 30 minutes. Dimple top with fingers and drizzle with melted butter. Sprinkle top evenly with brown sugar and cinnamon. Set aside and let rise again for 30 minutes. Preheat oven to 375 degrees. Bake 12 to 15 minutes. Remove to rack to cool.
Yield: 16 servings

Bethlehem, Pennsylvania, settled by Moravians in 1741, is known as the Christmas City. It is also well known for this unusual sugary cake. One of our winter residents shares her famous hometown recipe.

SLOVENIAN POTIKA

"My Slovenian mother-in-law was blessed with a fine baker's hand. Her Potika was ahead of its time with the abundance of chocolate in the filling."

1 package active dry yeast
1/4 cup warm water
1 cup milk, scalded
1/4 cup granulated sugar
1/4 cup butter
1 teaspoon salt
3 1/2 to 3 3/4 cups sifted all-purpose flour, divided
2 egg yolks

Filling
6 tablespoons light cream, scalded
2 cups chopped walnuts
3 (1-ounce) squares unsweetened chocolate, grated
2/3 cup granulated sugar
1/2 teaspoon salt
1/2 teaspoon vanilla extract
2 tablespoons butter
2 tablespoons fresh bread crumbs
1 egg white

Dissolve yeast in warm water. In large bowl, combine scalded milk, sugar, butter and salt. Cool to lukewarm and stir in 2 cups flour. Beat in yeast, egg yolks and enough remaining flour to make soft dough. Turn out on lightly floured surface, cover with towel and let stand 10 minutes.

Knead dough about 8 to 10 minutes or until smooth and elastic. Place in lightly greased bowl, turning to grease both sides. Cover with towel and let rise in draft-free area about 1 1/2 hours or until doubled. Punch down, and let rise about 45 minutes or until doubled once more.

While dough is rising, make filling. Add walnuts, chocolate, sugar, salt and vanilla to scalded cream. Blend well. In small sauté pan, melt butter and lightly brown bread crumbs. Add to cream mixture. Beat egg white until stiff and fold into mixture. Set aside.

Preheat oven to 375 degrees. Grease or spray 10-inch bundt pan. Turn dough onto lightly floured board and roll as thinly as possible. Lightly spoon nut filling over dough, spreading evenly almost to the edges. Roll up like jelly roll and place, seamside down, in prepared pan. Bake in middle rack of oven about 1 hour, testing after 45 minutes. Cool on rack.

Yield: 12 servings

SPICY APPLE HARVEST CAKE

1/2 cup butter, melted
2 cups granulated sugar
3 eggs, separated
2 teaspoons vanilla extract
3 cups cake flour, sifted
1 1/2 teaspoons baking soda
1/2 teaspoon salt
1/2 teaspoon cinnamon
1/8 teaspoon nutmeg
3 1/2 cups peeled, chopped apples
1 cup chopped walnuts

Preheat oven to 350 degrees. Grease or spray a 9-inch square baking pan.

In large mixer bowl, beat together butter, sugar, egg yolks, and vanilla. Sift together flour, baking soda, salt, cinnamon and nutmeg; stir into egg mixture. Add apples and walnuts; stir to distribute evenly. Beat egg whites until stiff; gently fold into batter. Spoon into prepared pan and bake 55 to 65 minutes or until done. Turn onto rack and cool. Cut in squares to serve.

Yield: 12 servings

A welcome treat that can be assembled in no time, especially if you have walnuts and apples on hand ... improves in flavor when made a day ahead.

NORWEGIAN KRINGLAR

"My mother, who was born in Norway, always included this traditional sweet, with the unique crust and creamy filling, in her holiday baskets for the family."

1 cup all-purpose flour
1/2 cup butter, chilled
1 to 2 tablespoons water
1 cup water
1/2 cup butter
1 cup all-purpose flour
3 eggs
1/2 teaspoon almond extract

Preheat oven to 350 degrees. Place flour in medium bowl and cut in butter until evenly distributed. Add just enough water to moisten, as for pie crust.

Roll dough out into 2 long strips about 3-inches wide. Place on lightly greased or sprayed cookie sheet.

Combine water and butter in saucepan and heat to boiling. Remove from heat and whisk in 1 cup flour, stirring until smooth. Add eggs one at a time, beating until smooth after each addition. Stir in almond extract. Spread mixture gently on pastry strips. Bake 30 minutes or until lightly browned and under crust is done. Cool on racks before frosting.

Frosting
1 cup confectioners' sugar
1 tablespoon light cream
1 tablespoon softened butter
1 teaspoon almond extract
1/4 cup raspberry or apricot jam
1 2/3 cup sliced almonds, toasted

Beat together sugar, cream, butter and almond extract. When smooth spread lightly over Kringlars. Heat jam, drizzle over frosting and sprinkle with toasted almonds. Yield: 16 servings

APPLE WALNUT STREUSEL

1 1/2 cups all-purpose flour
2 1/4 teaspoons baking powder
1/2 cup granulated sugar
1/2 teaspoon salt
1 teaspoon cinnamon
1 egg
1/2 cup milk
1/4 cup butter, melted
1 1/2 cups chopped apples
1/2 cup chopped walnuts

This traditional recipe is just perfect when the holiday pace is frantic yet the occasion calls for something special.

Streusel Topping
1/4 cup granulated sugar
2 tablespoons all-purpose flour
1/2 teaspoon cinnamon
1/2 teaspoon vanilla extract
1 tablespoon soft butter

Preheat oven to 400 degrees. Grease or spray an 8-inch square baking pan. Sift flour, measure and resift 3 times with next 4 ingredients. In large bowl, beat together egg, milk and melted butter. Gently stir in flour mixture. Fold in apples and walnuts. Spoon into prepared pan.

For topping, blend sugar, flour, cinnamon and vanilla. Work in butter until crumbly and sprinkle mixture evenly over batter. Bake 30 minutes or until toothpick, inserted in center, comes out clean.
Yield: 8 servings

TRADITIONAL SOUR CREAM
COFFEE CAKE

Just about everyone's favorite coffee cake ... simple, traditional, and delicious. But if you feel a wave of creativity coming on, you might add mini-chocolate chips, golden raisins, blueberries, or a mix of toasted coconut and walnuts.

1/2 cup butter

1 cup granulated sugar

2 eggs, lightly beaten

1 teaspoon baking soda

1 cup sour cream

1 1/2 cups sifted all-purpose flour

1 1/2 teaspoons baking powder

1 teaspoon vanilla extract

1/2 cup granulated sugar combined with

2 teaspoons cinnamon

Preheat oven to 350 degrees. Grease and flour 10-inch springform pan.

Cream butter, sugar and eggs together. Combine soda with sour cream and beat into egg mixture. Stir in flour and baking powder, mixing until smooth; add vanilla. Pour half of batter into prepared pan. Sprinkle half of sugar-cinnamon mixture over batter and swirl in with knife blade. Add remainder of batter, remainder of sugar-cinnamon mixture and repeat swirling motion. Bake 45 to 50 minutes. Turn off heat, open oven door and leave to cool 1 hour. Yield: 12 servings

SEA ISLAND MUFFINS

2 cups granulated sugar
1 cup whole wheat flour
3 cups all-purpose flour
2 tablespoons cinnamon
1/2 teaspoon nutmeg
1/2 teaspoon allspice
4 teaspoons baking soda
1 teaspoon salt
4 cups shredded carrots
2 cups shredded apples
1 cup raisins
6 eggs
1 cup canola oil
1/2 cup orange juice
1 teaspoon vanilla extract.

Originally from Nantucket, these healthy little gems have flourished on all the sea islands, including Hilton Head.

In large bowl, mix together sugar and whole wheat flour. Combine remaining dry ingredients and sift into sugar mixture; stir to combine. Stir in carrots, apples and raisins.

In another bowl beat together eggs, oil, orange juice and vanilla. Stir into dry ingredients, mixing gently until flour is just combined. Cover and refrigerate 24 hours to allow flavors to blend.

Preheat oven to 375 degrees. Grease or spray standard muffin pans. Fill two-thirds full with batter. Bake 20 to 25 minutes or until done.
Yield: 36 medium muffins or 24 large

BOUNCEBERRY MUFFINS

In the early years of cultivation, cranberries were also known as bounceberries, because they bounce when ripe.

2 cups all-purpose flour
1 cup whole wheat flour
3 teaspoons baking powder
1 teaspoon salt
1 teaspoon cinnamon
1 cup granulated sugar
2/3 cup butter, melted and cooled
1 cup buttermilk
2 eggs
2 cups fresh cranberries, halved
Grated peel of 1 lemon
4 tablespoons all-purpose flour

Topping
1/2 teaspoon cinnamon combined with
3 tablespoons granulated sugar

Preheat oven to 375 degrees. Spray standard muffin pans or insert paper liners.

In large bowl, combine dry ingredients. In separate smaller bowl, mix together buttermilk and eggs. Toss cranberries and lemon peel with 4 tablespoons flour.

Stir egg mixture into dry ingredients, mixing just until flour disappears. Gently stir in cranberry mixture. Do not over stir; batter should be a little lumpy.

Fill prepared pans two-thirds full. Sprinkle sugar-cinnamon mixture over muffins. Bake 20 to 25 minutes or until done. Cool 5 minutes before serving.

Yield: 16 muffins

MINCEMEAT MUFFINS

1 3/4 cups all-purpose flour

1/4 cup packed dark brown sugar

2 teaspoons baking powder

1/4 teaspoon baking soda

1/4 teaspoon salt

3/4 cup milk

1/4 cup unsalted butter, melted

1 egg

1 cup mincemeat

The subtle spice of mincemeat adds a surprising depth of flavor to these muffins.

Preheat oven to 375 degrees. Grease 12-cup muffin pan or insert paper liners. In large bowl, mix flour, brown sugar, baking powder, baking soda and salt. In another bowl, whisk together milk, melted butter and egg. Stir milk mixture gently into dry ingredients mixing just until moistened. Gently fold in mincemeat. Fill prepared muffin pan two-thirds full. Bake 15 to 20 minutes or until done.

Cook's Note: A term often encountered in baking is "until done." To test for doneness press top surface of baked item with finger tips. It should spring back leaving no imprint. Or you may insert a toothpick in center which will be clean when withdrawn.
Yield: 12 muffins

BUTTERMILK
CURRANT SCONES

Biscuit-tender and flecked with sweet black currants, these scones are best served hot from the oven ...with a tart citrus marmalade.

2 cups all-purpose flour
1/4 cup cake flour
1 tablespoon granulated sugar
2 1/4 teaspoons baking powder
1/2 teaspoon baking soda
1/2 teaspoon salt
1 1/2 teaspoons grated orange peel
1/2 cup cold butter, cubed
2/3 cup currants
1/2 cup plus 1 tablespoon buttermilk
1 egg, lightly beaten

Preheat oven to 425 degrees. Place oven rack in middle or slightly above.

In large bowl, mix together flours, sugar, baking powder, soda, salt and orange peel. With pastry blender (or 2 knives) cut butter into dry ingredients until mixture resembles coarse crumbs. Blend in currants. Add buttermilk all at once, stirring gently with a fork to make soft, slightly sticky dough. Do not overwork.

With floured hands, form dough into ball and place on floured surface. Knead gently 10 times. Pat dough into round 1/2-inch high. With 2 1/2-inch cookie cutter, cut as many scones as possible. Gather scraps, reform dough, and cut additional scones. Place on ungreased cookie sheet. Lightly brush tops with beaten egg. Bake 12 to 15 minutes or until golden.
Yield: 8 to 10 scones

Cheese Scone Variation: Eliminate sugar, peel and currants. To dry ingredients add: 1/4 teaspoon cayenne, 1/8 teaspoon dry mustard and 1 tablespoon poppy seeds. After cutting in butter, add 3/4 cup grated, sharp cheddar cheese. Proceed as above.

ZUCCHINI PINEAPPLE BREAD

3 eggs
1 cup vegetable oil
2 cups granulated sugar
2 teaspoons vanilla extract
2 cups shredded unpeeled zucchini
1 (20-ounce) can crushed pineapple, well-drained
3 cups all-purpose flour
2 teaspoons baking soda
2 teaspoons baking powder
1 teaspoon salt
1 1/2 teaspoons cinnamon
3/4 teaspoon nutmeg
1 cup coarsely chopped walnuts
1 cup seedless raisins

Needs no embellishment ... like most quick breads, just slice and serve.

Preheat oven to 350 degrees. Grease and flour two (9 x 5 x 3-inch) loaf pans. In large mixing bowl, beat eggs and stir in oil, sugar and vanilla. Gently stir in zucchini and crushed pineapple. In separate bowl sift together flour, baking powder, soda, salt, cinnamon and nutmeg. Blend in walnuts and raisins. Gently stir zucchini and pineapple into flour mixture just until mixed.

Spoon into prepared loaf pans. Bake 1 hour or until done. Remove from oven, cool 10 minutes in pan before transferring to cooling rack to cool completely. Wrap and refrigerate until needed. Yield: 2 loaves

This easy holiday bread

has it all

... fruit, nuts, spices,

and it freezes well.

PUMPKIN DATE-NUT BREAD

1 cup unsalted butter, softened

2 cups packed brown sugar

2 eggs

1 cup canned pumpkin

1 teaspoon vanilla extract

1/4 cup water

2 1/4 cups all-purpose flour

1 1/2 teaspoons baking powder

3/4 teaspoon cinnamon

1/2 teaspoon freshly ground nutmeg

1/2 teaspoon ground cloves

1/2 teaspoon salt

1 pound pitted and chopped dates, tossed with

1/4 cup all-purpose flour

1/2 cup chopped pecans

Preheat oven to 350 degrees. Grease and flour
3 (9 x 5 x 3-inch) loaf pans. In mixer bowl, cream
butter and brown sugar until light and fluffy. Add
eggs one at a time, beating well after each addition.
Add pumpkin, vanilla and water beating at medium
speed until well blended.

Sift flour, baking powder, spices and salt together.
Add gradually to egg mixture, beating until dough is
smooth. Stir in dates and pecans. Dough will be stiff.
Spoon into prepared pans. Bake 1 hour, or until
golden brown. Cool 10 minutes in pans before
removing to cooling racks.

Yield: 3 loaves

BREAD MACHINE PANETTONE

3 cups white bread flour
3/4 teaspoon salt
2 teaspoons gluten, optional
1 tablespoon flax seed
Grated zest from 1 large orange
2 tablespoons dry milk powder
3 tablespoons honey
4 tablespoons soft butter
2 eggs
4 tablespoons rum or marsala
1 tablespoon vanilla extract
1/4 cup water, approximately (see Cook's Note)
1/3 cup light raisins
1/3 cup dark raisins
1 1/2 teaspoons active dry yeast

Milanese sweet bread, beautifully packaged in gold foil and sold in gourmet shops, is a Christmas specialty. With your bread machine, you can easily produce this fruit filled loaf at home. Some say it tastes even better toasted.

Place all ingredients except raisins in bread machine pan. Program for Basic bread unless machine has special cycle for sweet or raisin breads. Press start. If dough appears very wet after 10 minutes of kneading, add 1 or 2 tablespoons more flour. When first kneading is complete, add raisins and complete cycle.
Yield: 1 loaf

Cook's Note: About measuring liquid ingredients: place eggs, rum or marsala and vanilla in measuring cup; fill to 1 cup level with water.

RENOWNED SPORTS TRADITIONS

Living on Hilton Head is an outdoor experience. The list of activities is endless. But it is golf and tennis that are responsible for Hilton Head's international sports acclaim.

The first Ocean golf course opened in 1961 in Sea Pines Plantation, and the game caught on like wildfire. In 1969, HarbourTown Links was inaugurated and the Heritage Classic was born. The Thanksgiving theme was an important part of our first four Heritage tournaments, all being played Thanksgiving week.

Today the PGA-sponsored tournament, MCI Classic - The Heritage of Golf, is played in April and is the key event on the Island sports calendar. It is attended by several thousand spectators and seen by hundreds of thousands on television.

The colorful Scottish bagpipe opening parade ... the opening cannon blast as the prior winner drives his ball into Calibogue Sound ... the champagne and general festivity and glamour surrounding the whole affair ... are part of the fabric of Island life.

If the Heritage is the star of the golfing year here, then the other 20 Island and 12 off-Island courses are the frosting on the cake. The roster of artists who designed these courses includes Pete Dye, Jack Nicklaus, Arnold Palmer, and Davis Love III.

Tennis takes no back seat when it comes to championship play. One of the leading tournaments in women's tennis, the Family Circle Magazine Cup with a million dollar purse, fills Sea Pines Tennis Stadium for a week.

Top-seeded players such as Graf and Seles arrive here and Chris Evert Lloyd returns each year as a sportscaster.

Our highly acclaimed Van der Meer Tennis University attracts 15,000 amateurs and 500 pros to Hilton Head each year. We have 360 other Island Tennis courts and 4 clubs listed in the top fifty in the country.

For premier golf and tennis ... the place to be is Hilton Head Island.

HE CHRISTMAS COOKIE JAR

page 191

If the kitchen is the heart of the home,

isn't the Cookie Jar the heart of the kitchen?

Especially, during Yuletide when baking days are

more than filling the cookie jar ...

they are also filling cooks of all ages

with the spirit of Christmas.

AUSTRIAN CRESCENTS

1 package dry yeast
3 cups all-purpose flour
1 cup butter, softened
3 egg yolks
1 (8-ounce) carton sour cream
1/2 cup granulated sugar
1/2 cup chopped pecans
3/4 teaspoon ground cinnamon
1 cup confectioners' sugar
3 tablespoons milk or water

Preheat oven to 350 degrees. Lightly butter 2 cookie sheets. Set aside. Combine yeast and flour in bowl; add butter, cut in, and mix well. Beat egg yolks into sour cream and stir into flour mixture. Mix with wooden spoon to form dough. Knead dough until smooth. Divide into 6 balls; wrap each in plastic. Refrigerate overnight.

Combine sugar, pecans and cinnamon. Set aside. Working with one ball of dough at a time, place on lightly floured surface and roll into 1/4-inch thick circle. Spread one-sixth sugar mixture evenly on the circle; cut into 16 wedges. Beginning at wide end, roll each wedge toward point. Pinch to seal points, and shape into crescents. Repeat with remaining balls of dough. Place on cookie sheet, point side down. Bake 18 minutes or until lightly browned. Transfer to racks to cool and drizzle with glaze while still warm.

To make glaze, stir together 1 cup confectioners' sugar and 3 tablespoons milk or water until mixture reaches glazing consistency.
Yield: 8 dozen cookies

Nothing puts you in the holiday spirit more than baking that first batch of Christmas cookies… this is a great one to start with.

PORT ROYAL BENNE WAFERS

Only in the South Carolina Lowcountry are sesame seeds referred to as benne seeds. The people of the upper Niger River Valley brought the seeds here aboard African slave ships. Initially, because of their scarcity, they were reserved only for holiday baking.

1/2 cup sesame seeds
1/2 cup butter, softened
1 cup granulated sugar
1/2 teaspoon vanilla extract
1 egg
1 3/4 cups all-purpose flour
1/4 teaspoon salt
1/2 teaspoon baking soda
1 1/2 teaspoons baking powder

Preheat oven to 350 degrees. On cookie sheet, toast sesame seeds for 15 minutes, shaking from time to time, until golden. Remove seeds and cool.

Cream butter and sugar together in mixing bowl. Beat vanilla extract and egg into butter mixture. Sift together flour, salt, baking soda and baking powder. Add to butter mixture; mix well. Blend in sesame seeds. Place dough in plastic wrap and refrigerate for 1 hour.

Preheat oven to 325 degrees. Butter 2 cookie sheets. Pinch pieces of dough into small balls. Place on prepared cookie sheets and flatten with fingertips until the dough is as thin as possible, about 2-inch rounds.

Bake 10 minutes or until golden brown. Cool on pans for just a minute; carefully remove to cooling racks. Repeat process and store in airtight containers.
Yield: 6 dozen cookies

SCOTTISH SHORTBREAD

1 cup butter at room temperature
1/2 cup super-fine granulated sugar
2 cups, less 2 tablespoons, all-purpose flour
2 tablespoons rice flour

Preheat oven to 300 degrees.

Cream butter and sugar together until very light.
Work in two-thirds of the flour and all of the rice
flour. On floured board knead in remaining flour.
Continue kneading until dough is smooth and just
cracks at the edges. Roll dough out with floured
rolling pin to a thickness of 1/4-inch. Cut into desired
shapes using Christmas cookie cutters.

Bake on ungreased cookie sheets 20 to 25 minutes or
until very lightly colored. Cool on racks. Store in
tightly covered tins.
Yield: 3 dozen cookies

*"I met Mrs. MacGowan
on a train to
Glasgow. At tea the
next afternoon, she
served this marvelous
shortbread. While
shortbread recipes vary
regionally in Scotland,
this one remains
my favorite."*

HOLLY'S WHIPPED SHORTBREAD

These melt-in-your-mouth cookies may be decorated with cherries, nuts or ginger, depending on the season.

1 cup confectioners' sugar
2 cups butter, softened
3 cups all-purpose flour

Preheat oven to 350 degrees. In large mixer bowl, combine sugar, butter and flour. Beat together until thoroughly blended at medium speed. Continue to beat at high speed for 10 minutes or until the consistency of whipped cream. Drop by teaspoonsful onto ungreased cookie sheets. Bake 10 to 15 minutes or until golden. Yield: 5 dozen cookies

BRANDY SNAPS

After rolling a few you'll get the hang of it. For an added touch, fill with whipped cream, flavored with a hint of brandy, just before serving.

3/4 cup butter
3/4 cup granulated sugar
1/2 cup molasses
2 teaspoons ground ginger
1 1/2 cups sifted all-purpose flour
2 teaspoons grated lemon rind
1 teaspoon brandy

Preheat oven to 300 degrees. Butter cookie sheets. In a medium pan, melt butter; add granulated sugar and molasses. Stir until sugar has dissolved. Add ground ginger. Remove from heat and add flour in small batches, mixing well after each addition. Add lemon rind and brandy. Stir well.

Drop batter by spoonsful onto prepared pan, 2 inches apart. Bake 12 minutes. Remove from oven. Carefully lift cookies from pan and drape over handle of a wooden spoon. If cookies become too hard to handle, return briefly to hot oven until softened. Can be baked days in advance, and stored in airtight tins. Yield: 4 dozen cookies

RUSSIAN WHITE CHRISTMAS COOKIES

2 cups butter, at room temperature
1 cup confectioners' sugar
2 teaspoons vanilla extract
4 1/2 cups all-purpose flour
1/2 teaspoon salt
2 cups finely chopped walnuts

Preheat oven to 350 degrees. In mixer bowl, cream together butter, sugar and vanilla. Sift together flour and salt. Mix into creamed mixture.

Form into 3/4-inch balls and place on ungreased cookie sheets.

Bake 15 to 17 minutes. Roll in confectioners' sugar while still hot. When cookies are cool, roll once more in confectioners' sugar. Store for up to a month in airtight Christmas tins.
Yield: 6 dozen cookies

A rich butter cookie known by many different names around the world and always delicious.

LEMON KISS SURPRISE

1 1/2 cups butter, softened
3/4 cups granulated sugar
1 tablespoon lemon extract
2 3/4 cups all-purpose flour
1 1/2 cups finely chopped almonds
1 (14-ounce) package chocolate-almond candy kisses
Confectioners' sugar, for dusting cookies

In large mixer bowl, cream butter, sugar and lemon extract until light and fluffy. Add flour and almonds; beat until well blended. Cover and refrigerate at least one hour.

Preheat oven to 375 degrees. Shape scant tablespoon of dough around each chocolate-almond kiss and roll into a ball. As cookies are formed, place them on ungreased cookie sheets and bake 8 to 12 minutes or until bottom edges are golden brown. Cool, and remove from cookie sheet. Dust with confectioners' sugar.
Yield: 6 dozen cookies

Delightful bitefuls! The surprise comes with the first kiss.

CANDY CANE CRISPS

*Christmas comes
and Christmas goes
but candy canes linger
until they become
dessert.*

1 cup butter
1 cup confectioners' sugar, unsifted
1 1/2 teaspoons vanilla extract
1 1/3 cups all-purpose flour, spooned to measure
1 cup rolled oats
1/2 teaspoon salt
3/4 cup coarsely crushed candy canes, divided
Confectioners' sugar, for rolling cookies

Preheat oven to 325 degrees. Lightly butter, or line with parchment, 2 cookie sheets. Set aside.

Cream together butter and confectioners' sugar. Stir in vanilla, flour, oats and salt; mix thoroughly. Stir in 1/4 cup of the crushed candy canes. Roll rounded teaspoons of dough into 3/4-inch balls; roll each in confectioner's sugar. Place 2-inches apart on cookie sheets. Flatten with fork, making crisscross pattern. Sprinkle each cookie with 1/2 teaspoon of remaining crushed candy canes. Bake 18 to 20 minutes.
Lift cookies with metal spatula and transfer to racks to cool.
Yield: 2 1/2 dozen cookies

Cook's Note: When spraying cookie sheets, muffin tins, and baking pans, place them on open door of dishwasher. Excess spray is quickly washed away when you run the dishwasher.

CHRISTMAS LACE COOKIES

2 1/2 cups rolled oats
1 pound light brown sugar
3 tablespoons all-purpose flour
1 egg, beaten
1 cup melted butter
1 teaspoon vanilla extract
4 (1-ounce) semisweet chocolate squares

Preheat oven to 375 degrees. Line 2 cookie sheets with parchment paper.

In large bowl, with wooden spoon, mix together rolled oats, brown sugar and flour. Add egg, butter and vanilla. Stir until well combined. Drop batter by teaspoonsful, 2-inches apart, onto prepared cookie sheets.

Bake 8 minutes. Cool. Carefully remove cookies with metal spatula to tea towel. Meanwhile, melt chocolate. Dip half of each cookie in chocolate. Place on cooling racks to dry.
Yield: 3 dozen cookies

Brush the backs of these elegant cookies with melted chocolate and they are transformed into Florentines.

JANE'S FRUITCAKE COOKIES

While cookies are still hot, brush them with hot corn syrup and they will glow like Christmas ornaments. This method works with all fruitcakes.

1/2 cup butter

2 cups light brown sugar

1 cup whiskey

4 eggs

3 1/2 cups all-purpose flour

1 teaspoon soda

I teaspoon nutmeg

1 teaspoon cinnamon

1 1/2 pounds chopped nuts

1 1/2 pounds light and dark raisins

8 ounces red glacé cherries

8 ounces green glacé cherries

Cream butter and sugar together; beat in eggs and whiskey. Sift dry ingredients together and gradually mix into butter mixture. Fold in nuts, raisins and cherries. Refrigerate overnight.

Preheat oven to 350 degrees. Spray cookie sheet with baking spray or line with parchment paper. Drop cookies by teaspoonsful onto cookie sheet. Bake 10 to 12 minutes. Cool on racks; store in airtight containers. Yield: 7 dozen cookies

FRUIT FILLED SPRITZ COOKIES

1 cup butter
1 cup granulated sugar
1/2 cup packed brown sugar
3 eggs
1/2 teaspoon vanilla extract
1/2 teaspoon almond extract
4 cups all-purpose flour
1/2 teaspoon baking soda
1/2 teaspoon salt

Filling
1 cup water
1/2 cup granulated sugar
2 teaspoons grated orange rind
1 3/4 cups finely chopped glacé cherries
1/2 cup coconut
1 cup chopped nuts
Confectioners' sugar, for dusting

Made with a special press, these German cookies are called "Spritz"... a German word meaning "to squirt"... well worth the time it takes to make them.

To prepare cookie dough, cream butter and sugar until light. Beat in eggs and extracts. Sift together dry ingredients and add gradually to creamed mixture. Chill 2 hours or overnight.

To prepare filling, combine ingredients listed; set aside until ready to assemble the cookies.

When ready to bake, preheat oven to 375 degrees. Do not grease baking sheet. Spoon and pack cookie dough into cookie press with saw-tooth plate, or into a super shooter. Press dough in strips across width of baking sheet. Spread each strip of dough with prepared filling. Cover with second strip of dough. Bake 12 to 15 minutes, or until lightly browned. Cut strips into 2-inch bars and remove to cooling rack. Dust cookies with confectioners' sugar.
Yield: 6 dozen cookies

CLASSIC RAISIN SPICE COOKIES

*...when the house is
perfumed with these
spices, the anticipation of
Christmas is almost
intoxicating!*

3 cups all-purpose flour
1 teaspoon soda
1 teaspoon salt
2 teaspoons ground cinnamon
1 teaspoon ground cloves
1 cup shortening
1 1/2 cups packed light brown sugar
3 eggs
1 teaspoon vanilla extract
3 cups seedless raisins

Glaze
3 cups sifted confectioners' sugar
3 to 4 tablespoons milk
1 teaspoon vanilla extract

Preheat oven to 350 degrees. Spray or grease two cookie sheets.

Sift flour, soda, salt, cinnamon and cloves together. Set aside. In large mixer bowl, at medium speed, cream together shortening, sugar, eggs and vanilla.

Beat in flour mixture at low speed until well combined. Stir in raisins. Drop batter by teaspoonsful onto prepared cookie sheet. Bake 10 to 12 minutes.

Cool cookies on racks. Combine ingredients for glaze and drizzle over cookies.
Yield: 5 dozen cookies

LEBKUCHEN
(MOLASSES SPICE COOKIES)

1 cup shortening
1 cup butter
4 cups dark molasses
1 1/2 tablespoons baking soda, dissolved in water
2 cups packed dark brown sugar
6 eggs
Rind and juice of 1 lemon
2 teaspoons each: ground cinnamon, cloves, nutmeg and ginger
1/2 teaspoon each: ground cardamom seeds and ground star anise
5 to 6 cups all-purpose flour
2 cups currants or chopped raisins
1/2 cup citron, minced

Preheat oven to 350 degrees. Melt butter and shortening in sauce pan over moderate heat, transfer to large mixing bowl. Add molasses and baking soda to mixture. Beat in brown sugar and eggs. Stir in lemon juice and rind.

Sift together spices and 5 cups of the flour; stir into molasses mixture until dough becomes quite stiff. Dust citron and currants or raisins with part of remaining flour, and work into cookie dough. Work in as much remaining flour as possible.

Flour a board, divide dough into manageable pieces and roll each out to thickness of 1/8-inch. With knife, cut dough into rectangular shapes about 1 x 3-inches. Bake on ungreased cookie sheets about 15 minutes. Transfer to racks to cool.
Yield: 8 dozen cookies

"My mother began making cookies weeks before Christmas. But it was my Dad and I who got to deliver them to friends and neighbors ... often on snow covered roads. We called them Lebkuchen then, and they take me back there now."

COCONUT MINCEMEAT BARS

The first recorded recipe for mincemeat dates back to 1846. This traditional British Christmas fare, usually found in pies and tarts, is right at home in this delicious bar cookie.

1 1/2 cups all-purpose flour
1 cup granulated sugar
3/4 cup cold butter, in small cubes
1/2 cup chopped nuts
1 1/2 cups flaked sweetened coconut
3/4 cup prepared mincemeat
3 tablespoons brandy or whiskey

Preheat oven to 325 degrees. Butter a 9 x 13 x 2-inch pan. Mix flour, sugar and butter with pastry blender or fingers. Add nuts and coconut. Spoon half the mixture into prepared pan. Combine mincemeat and brandy; spoon over flour mixture to within a half-inch of edge of pan. Sprinkle remaining flour and nut mixture over mincemeat.

Bake 40 minutes. Cool and cut into bars to serve. These bars freeze well.
Yield: 2 dozen bars

MINCEMEAT
ALMOND DIAMONDS

3/4 cup butter
2/3 cup granulated sugar
1 egg
1 teaspoon almond extract
2 1/2 cups sifted all-purpose flour
1/2 teaspoon salt
1/2 teaspoon cinnamon
1 to 1 1/2 cups prepared mincemeat
1 egg, beaten with 1 tablespoon water
1/3 cup chopped blanched almonds
2 tablespoons granulated sugar

...not only shaped like diamonds, these bar cookies sparkle like diamonds when the sugar topping melts to form a glaze.

Preheat oven to 350 degrees. Cream butter, sugar, egg and almond extract together. Sift together flour, salt and cinnamon. Add dry ingredients to creamed mixture and stir until well blended. Cover and chill briefly.

Divide dough in half. Roll out first half on lightly greased rimless cooking sheet to form an 8 x 10-inch rectangle. Spread mincemeat evenly over dough leaving space on outer edges.

Roll out second half of dough between sheets of wax paper. Remove top sheet of wax paper, and invert dough over mincemeat layer. Remove second sheet of wax paper. Press to seal edges. Brush with egg wash and sprinkle with chopped almonds, followed by granulated sugar.

Bake 25 to 30 minutes, or until lightly browned. Cool and cut into small diamond-shaped bar cookies.
Yield: 16 to 18 cookies

MERRY MANDELBROT

This Jewish favorite is a crisp almond bread eaten as a cookie. Great for dipping with eggnog, hot chocolate, or a light semi-sweet Moscato wine.

1/2 cup butter, at room temperature
1 cup granulated sugar
2 eggs
1 teaspoon vanilla extract
2 cups all-purpose flour
1 teaspoon baking powder
3/4 cup chopped nuts (almonds, pecans or walnuts)
1 cup semisweet chocolate chips

Preheat oven to 350 degrees and butter or spray 2 cookie sheets. In large mixer bowl, cream butter, sugar, eggs and vanilla together. Sift flour and baking powder into creamed mixture while beating on low speed. Stir in nuts. Form mixture into 4 rectangular bars on cookie sheets. Bake 20 minutes. Remove from oven. Increase oven temperature to 400 degrees.

With bread knife cut mandelbrots into 1/2-inch slices. Return slices to cookie sheet and toast, turning once, until lightly browned on both sides. Remove to rack to cool.

Meanwhile, melt chocolate over gentle heat. Dip one side of sliced mandelbrot into melted chocolate, and place on wax paper to set.
Yield: 3 dozen slices

GINGER BISCOTTI

1/2 cup sweet butter, softened
1/4 cup molasses
3/4 cup dark brown sugar
1/2 teaspoon vanilla
2 teaspoons grated orange peel
2 eggs at room temperature
2 3/4 cups all-purpose flour
3/4 teaspoon baking soda
1 1/2 teaspoons ground ginger
1 teaspoon ground cinnamon
1/2 teaspoon freshly grated nutmeg
Pinch ground cloves

Cinnamon, nutmeg and ginger scented, these twice-baked crisp cookies will fill your house with their wonderful aroma. They're incredible with cappuccino.

Preheat oven to 350 degrees. Lightly grease or spray 2 cookie sheets. In large mixer bowl, cream together butter, molasses and brown sugar. Mix in vanilla and orange peel. Add eggs one at a time, beating well after each addition. In separate bowl sift together flour, baking soda, salt and spices. Stir gently into sugar mixture until just combined. Do not over mix.

Divide dough into thirds. With hands shape each third into log 10 inches long, 2 inches wide, no more than 1-inch high. Arrange on baking sheets 3 inches apart. Bake on middle rack of oven 20 minutes, or until top is cracked and crevices appear dry. Remove from oven and cool on racks 10 minutes.

On cutting board, cut loaves crosswise, on diagonal, into 3/4-inch slices. Stand slices upright, without touching, on cookie sheets. Return to oven and bake 10 minutes or until dry and lightly browned. Remove to racks to cool. Keep in airtight containers at room temperature, or freeze. Do not refrigerate.
Yield: 40 biscotti

NOEL BERRY'S
YULETIDE COOKIES

'The First Noël' takes on

new meaning …

mincemeat,

cardamom, and rum…

something to sing about.

1 cup shortening

1 1/2 cups granulated sugar

3 eggs

3 cups all-purpose flour

1 teaspoon baking soda

1/2 (scant) teaspoon salt

1 (20 1/2-ounce) jar mincemeat

1/4 cup thick marmalade

3/4 teaspoon cinnamon

1/4 teaspoon ground cardamom

1/4 cup finely chopped walnuts

2 tablespoons dark rum

Preheat oven to 375 degrees. Prepare cookie sheets with baking spray or line with parchment paper.

In large mixer bowl, cream shortening, sugar and eggs until light. Sift flour, soda and salt together; on low speed, gradually beat into egg mixture. Combine mincemeat, marmalade, spices, walnuts and rum. Stir into cookie batter until fully combined.

Drop by teaspoonsful, 2 inches apart, onto cookie sheet. Bake 10 to 12 minutes or until lightly browned. Yield: 7 dozen cookies

OLD-FASHIONED
SUGAR COOKIES

1/3 cup butter at room temperature
1/3 cup shortening
3/4 cup granulated sugar
1 teaspoon baking powder
1/4 teaspoon salt
1 tablespoon milk
2 teaspoons vanilla extract
1/4 teaspoon lemon extract
1 egg
2 1/4 cups all-purpose flour

These are the cookies that Christmas memories are made of … just like Grandma used to make with you. The dough is perfect for cutting into all kinds of fanciful shapes.

In large mixer bowl, at med-high speed, beat butter and shortening until creamy, about 2 minutes. Add sugar, baking powder and salt; beat until light and fluffy. Reduce mixer speed to low; add milk, flavorings and egg, and beat until well combined. Mix in 2 cups of flour until well blended. If dough seems a little soft, add up to 1/4 cup flour.

Divide dough in half; wrap each well in plastic, flatten slightly and chill at least 3 hours or overnight. Preheat oven to 350 degrees. Roll half of dough on lightly floured surface to 1/8-inch thickness. With 3-to 4-inch floured, assorted cookie cutters, cut dough into as many shapes as possible. Place cut-outs 1-inch apart on ungreased cookie sheets. Gather up trimmings and reroll for more cookies.

Bake on racks in oven, rotating position once, 10 to 12 minutes or until edges just begin to color. Cool on wire racks. Decorate if desired with royal icing (p. 223) and colored sprinkles.
Yield: 3 dozen cookies

GERMAN SPRINGERLE COOKIES

Seek out a friend who has inherited a well-seasoned springerle mold, and share the Yuletide experience of making these together.

4 eggs
1 teaspoon oil of anise
1 pound confectioners' sugar
2/3 teaspoon baking powder
1/4 teaspoon salt
3 1/2 to 4 cups all-purpose flour
Springerle Cookie Mold (3 1/2 x 4 1/2-inches, 4 designs)

In large mixer bowl, beat eggs until thick and light in color. Add oil of anise. Gradually add confectioners' sugar while continuing to beat on high speed. Sift together 1 1/2 cups of flour, baking powder and salt. Beat into egg mixture. Slowly add remaining flour until dough becomes so thick that it stops beaters. Remove dough to board and knead in remainder of flour, if any. Shape into log, approximately 2 inches in diameter.

From the log, cut slice of dough; roll to thickness of 1/4-inch. Lay rolled dough on springerle mold which has been dusted with flour. With fingers, press dough gently into designs. Trim away excess with knife. Invert mold and let imprinted dough fall onto your hand. Transfer to wax paper. Cut designs apart with knife. Continue process, using all cookie dough. Let cookies dry overnight, uncovered.

Preheat oven to 350 degrees. Place cookies on lightly greased cookie sheets. Bake 12 to 15 minutes or until dry. Cool and store in airtight container.
Yield: 4 dozen cookies

Cook's Note: Apple slices placed in container will keep cookies fresh.

OATMEAL CRANBERRY COOKIES

1 1/2 cups all-purpose flour
1 teaspoon baking soda
1/2 cup butter
1/2 cup vegetable shortening
3/4 cup granulated sugar
3/4 cup brown sugar
1 egg
1 teaspoon vanilla extract
1 1/2 cups rolled oats
1 cup dried cranberries
1 cup butterscotch bits

Oatmeal cookies traditionally have raisins, but you can give them new holiday flavor with dried cranberries. Crunchy and delicious with a cold glass of milk.

Sift flour and baking soda together and set aside. In large mixer bowl, mix together butter and shortening. Beat in egg, vanilla, granulated and brown sugars until creamy in texture. Mix in flour mixture. Fold in rolled oats, cranberries and butterscotch bits. Shape into log. Wrap in plastic and chill 1 hour, or overnight.

Preheat oven to 350 degrees. Grease 2 cookie sheets. Slice dough into 1/2-inch rounds, place on cookie sheets, and bake 8 to 10 minutes. Remove to cooling racks.

Yield: 4 dozen cookies

OATMEAL CRISPS
FOR SANTA

This year, leave St. Nick a platter of these cookies and you'll probably find an extra goody in your stocking!

1 1/2 cups all-purpose flour
1 1/2 teaspoons baking soda
2 teaspoons baking powder
1 cup butter
1 1/2 cups brown sugar
1 egg, beaten
1 1/2 cups rolled oats
1 cup flaked sweetened coconut
1 cup chopped walnuts

Sift together flour, baking soda and baking powder; set aside. In large mixer bowl, cream butter and brown sugar together about 3 minutes, or until fluffy. Beat in egg. Add flour mixture to creamed mixture, beating on low speed until well combined. Stir in oats, coconut and walnuts. Cover and refrigerate 1 hour.

Preheat oven to 350 degrees. Lightly butter or spray 2 cookie sheets. Roll dough into walnut size balls. Place on cookie sheet about 2 inches apart. Flatten with fork. Bake 8 to 10 minutes. Cool briefly, before removing from cookie sheets to racks to cool completely.
Yield: 5 dozen cookies

PECAN MACAROONS

3 egg whites
1 1/3 cups superfine granulated sugar
1 1/4 cups all-purpose flour
2 teaspoons baking powder
1 teaspoon vanilla extract
2 cups finely chopped pecans (do not grind)

Preheat oven to 325 degrees. Line cookie sheets with parchment paper or grease lightly. Set aside.

Beat egg whites until light and fluffy. Beat in sugar gradually. Sift flour and baking powder together; fold into egg white mixture. Fold in vanilla and pecans. Drop by teaspoonsful onto prepared cookie sheets.

Bake 10 to 12 minutes or until beige in color. Cool on pan 5 minutes, before removing to racks to complete cooling. May be stored in tightly covered tins.
Yield: 40 cookies

Cook's Note: Superfine sugar may be made from granulated sugar by processing a few minutes in a blender or food processor.

We usually think of coconut or almonds when we think of macaroons , but one Hilton Head Island family has been making Christmas macaroons with pecans for over 100 years!

THE ISLAND WATERWAYS

The endless waterways, marshes, beaches, and wildlife of this Southeast coastal island offer vast diversity for those who live and vacation here.

Much of what is so special about Hilton Head is captured when exploring our waterways – on the Calibogue Sound, the Broad River, the Intracoastal Waterway, the Atlantic, or through winding channels of marsh. There is also an unusual system of ponds and lagoons here.

Our waters have produced bountiful harvests since early times. Native Americans, 18th and 19th century settlers, conquistadors, and confederates all relied on the sea and land for nourishment.

Hilton Head is a mecca for shrimping, whether casting a net from the shoreline, or dragging nets behind small boats. By wading in the shallow marshlands, clumps of choice oysters are harvested. Flat-bottomed bateaux usually come back to shore completely filled. Dangling a chicken neck at the end of a string, while crabbing off docks, will quickly fill a bucket with our famous blue crabs.

Surf fishermen cast for striped bass, bluefish and flounder. Boats can be chartered for deep-sea fishing, dolphin watching, or fishing around manmade reefs. Spanish mackerel, kings, cobia, and grouper are prized catches. Sixty miles out in the Gulf stream you are in marlin, sailfish, and barracuda waters.

Perhaps Hilton Head's greatest attraction is its talcum-soft beaches which stretch for twelve miles along the Atlantic ocean ... inviting sunbathing, walking, seashell admiring, picnics, and the best spot you could ever choose for reading your latest novel.

Another dimension to our waterways is a host of water sports: sailing, power cruising, wind surfing, kayaking, canoeing, and jet skiing.

Popular water-related challenges vary from the national Bluefish Tournament, to the Mumm's 30 World Championship Regatta, and the National Seniors Wind Surfing Cup.

Cruising the open waters, wrapped in the warmth of a glorious blue-skied afternoon or sailing through an evening filled with the fading colors of sunset and the silvery glow of moonlight, is an unforgetable experience.

KIDS IN THE KITCHEN

page 215

Cooking with kids

is a great family activity

and it's always been a parent-to-child thing.

Most of these recipes will require some parental guidance,

but many can be fully prepared

by the kids.

There's no better place to experience

the fun and meaning of the holidays

than in the kitchen.

This is where kids can learn to

care, share, and create

while loving every minute of it.

EGGS McCHRISTMAS

6 eggs
Tiny finger-pinch of salt and black pepper to season
6 thin slices deli-baked ham
1 tablespoon minced red bell pepper
1 tablespoon minced green bell pepper
4 English muffins
2 tablespoons butter, at room temperature
1/2 cup shredded pizza-mix cheese

The red and green peppers and a little spice put the Christmas spirit into most kids' breakfast favorite.

Ronald should approve!

To prepare this holiday treat, get everything ready before you start to cook. Break eggs into small mixing bowl and put in salt and pepper. Beat with fork until yolks and whites are well blended; set aside. Next, tear ham into small pieces; set aside.

Using a knife on a cutting board, cut red and green peppers into tiny, tiny cubes (this is called mincing). Then, using a fork, pierce edges of muffins and gently pull them apart. Toast muffins in the toaster and set aside.

Melt butter in frying pan over medium heat. Dump in red and green peppers and cook 1 minute. Next pour beaten eggs on top and stir with a wooden spoon. When eggs begin to thicken a little, sprinkle in ham and cheese. Cook, stirring gently, until eggs are firm and shiny, not dry. Spoon eggs on the 4 muffin bottoms. Cover with muffin top.
Yield: 4 servings

SAVORY CHRISTMAS WREATH PIZZA

Kids love to get their

hands into bread dough

and make a fun design

like this Christmas

wreath. Best of all they

love to eat everything

they create.

Olive oil
1 loaf frozen pizza dough, thawed
1 (8-ounce) can pizza sauce
1 small green bell pepper, sliced into thin rings
1 small red bell pepper, sliced into thin rings
1/2 cup sliced ripe olives
1/2 of (3 1/2-ounce) package thinly sliced pepperoni
1 1/2 cups grated mozzarella cheese

Preheat oven to 350 degrees. Wash your hands. Drizzle olive oil through your fingers and spread it on bottom and sides of 12-inch pizza pan. Put thawed dough on pizza pan. Stretch and pull dough with your fingers until bottom is covered, and it comes up the sides a little. Spread pizza sauce over dough with rubber spatula.

Make wreath 2 inches from outside rim by alternating red and green rings. Arrange olives decoratively on pepper rings. Lightly sprinkle mozzarella cheese over remaining exposed pizza sauce surface.

Bake on lowest rack in oven 25 to 30 minutes or until cheese is melted and light brown.
Yield: 4 to 6 servings

ALEX'S PIG-IN-A-WRAP

These peek-a-boo wraps

will put a new twist

on an old dog.

1 (16-ounce) package hot dogs
1/2 cup shredded cheddar cheese
3 tablespoons ketchup
2 tablespoons prepared mustard
2 (7-ounce) packages refrigerated breadstick dough

Preheat oven to 350 degrees. Split each hot dog, being careful not to cut all the way through. In small bowl, combine cheese, ketchup and mustard. Spoon into slit of each hot dog. Separate breadstick dough into 10 sections. Wind each bread section in spiral fashion around each hot dog. Place on baking sheet. Bake 15 to 18 minutes or until bread is golden. Let cool 5 minutes before biting into.

Yield: 10 servings

BEEF CUP-A-CAKES

2 tablespoons butter, at room temperature
1 medium size onion, chopped
1 1/2 pounds ground beef chuck
1/4 cup dried bread crumbs
1/2 teaspoon garlic powder
1 egg
1/4 teaspoon pepper
6 tablespoons ketchup
3 teaspoons prepared mustard

Mom may need to help with the knife, and also when the cup-a-cakes go in and out of the oven.

Wash your hands and then preheat oven to 350 degrees. Get out a 6-cup muffin tin and lightly butter each cup, using a paper napkin to spread the butter.

Next, place onion on cutting board. Using a small knife, trim off ends and then cut onion in half from end to end. Peel off skin and throw it away. Place onion halves flat side down on the board and cut lengthwise into several slices. Then cut across the slices to make small pieces. Put onion pieces into a small mixing bowl. Break up meat with your hands and let fall on top of onion. Add bread crumbs, garlic powder, salt and pepper. Break eggs in last. Now mix it all together.

Spoon 1 tablespoon ketchup into each of 6 buttered muffin cups, followed by 1/2 teaspoon mustard. Using your hands again, divide meat mixture evenly among 6 cups.

Place muffin tin on cookie sheet. Put on oven mitts and place cookie sheet in oven for 25 minutes. Then scoop out the little cakes and place them on a plate. Yield : 6 servings

"X"MAS STUFFED BAKED POTATOES

This one-dish meal served in a shell is a favorite for kids of all ages. It's a favorite for Mom too, because she knows it is rich in fiber, complex carbohydrates, potassium, and is a good source of vitamin C.

4 (8-ounce) russet baking potatoes
1 (10-ounce) package frozen broccoli in cheese sauce, partially thawed
1 (2-ounce) jar chopped pimientos
1 (2.25-ounce) can sliced black olives
1 teaspoon prepared mustard
4 parsley sprigs for garnish

Preheat oven to 375 degrees. Wash potatoes and pat dry with paper towel. Using a long-tined fork, poke potato on top and bottom several times. Rub skins lightly with shortening or oil and place on baking sheet, not touching.

Be careful when you use a hot oven, always using hot-pad mitts. Place baking sheet in oven and bake 1 hour, or until potatoes are tender when poked with a long-tined fork. While potatoes are baking, prepare topping. Place broccoli in cheese sauce in saucepan over medium heat and simmer until bubbly. Add pimientos, olives and mustard. Continue to cook another 3 to 4 minutes. Remove from burner and set aside.

After potatoes have baked for 1 hour, put on mitts and carefully remove hot tray. Cut a large "X" in top of each potato. With mitts still on, press on all sides to make center pop up like a volcano. Spoon broccoli mixture over potatoes and place parsley sprig on top of each one.

Yield: 4 servings

BEN'S CHRISTMAS SOUP
FROM A TO Z

…an educated soup…

or, learning

while the pot boils.

1 large onion, coarsely chopped
2 garlic cloves, chopped
2 tablespoons vegetable or olive oil
2 tablespoons mixed, dried Italian herb seasonings
1 (16-ounce) can stewed tomatoes with juice
4 cups canned beef broth
2 cups water
4 cups frozen mixed vegetables
1/2 cup alphabet pasta
1/2 teaspoon black pepper
Salt to taste
3 tablespoons minced fresh parsley

In a large soup pot, cook onion and garlic over medium heat until onion is golden, about 8 minutes. Add herb seasoning and cook, while stirring, for one minute. Wash your hands and squish the tomatoes through your hands as you add them to the pot. Add beef broth, then water and bring to boil. Reduce heat to medium and simmer (simmer means very low heat that makes tiny bubbles), for 10 minutes to blend flavors.

Add vegetables and alphabet pasta. Simmer, uncovered, over medium heat until they are both tender, 10 to 12 minutes. Season soup with pepper and salt, and stir in the parsley.
Yield: 8 servings

GINGERBREAD PEOPLE

This dough works well for tree or package ornament shapes. Use your favorite holiday cookie cutters and make a hole in the top of each cookie with a skewer before baking. The same dough also works well for making gingerbread houses.

5 cups all-purpose flour
1 1/2 teaspoons baking soda
1/2 teaspoon salt
1 teaspoon nutmeg
1 teaspoon ground cloves
2 teaspoon cinnamon
2 teaspoons ground ginger
1 cup vegetable shortening or butter
1 cup granulated sugar
1 1/2 cups molasses
2 eggs, beaten

Sift flour, soda and spices together and set aside. In large mixer bowl, cream together sugar and butter or shortening. Combine beaten eggs and molasses.

Gradually add flour mixture to creamed mixture, alternating with egg and molasses, until all flour is incorporated. Mix well. Cover dough and refrigerate overnight.

Preheat oven to 375 degrees. Line cookie sheets with parchment paper. Divide dough into 4 or 5 pieces; work with one piece at a time. On lightly floured board, roll out dough 1/8-inch thick. Cut into gingerbread boy and girl shapes with floured cookie cutters. Use raisins for making faces and for buttons on their tummies, if you like. Place cookies on prepared sheets and bake 10 minutes. Carefully remove to a cooling rack and cool completely before decorating or frosting with Royal Icing (recipe follows).
Yield: 3 1/2 dozen gingerbread people

Royal Icing

3 cups confectioners' sugar
2 tablespoons meringue powder (available in super-markets)
6 to 7 tablespoons warm water
Food coloring, as desired

... the perfect icing for giving some personality to your gingerbread people and houses.

In a clean, grease-free mixing bowl, combine sugar and meringue powder. Add water and beat until icing forms peaks; about 8 to 10 minutes. Keep icing covered with a damp cloth while in use and store in an airtight container. It does not need refrigeration. Reheat on low heat before using again.

When coloring icing, always use a little pigment at a time. (It's easy to add more color and very difficult to remove it.) When making batches of colored icing, always make a generous amount as it is very difficult to duplicate a shade.
Yield: 3 cups

MICHELLE'S ONE-BOWL
BROWNIES

1/2 cup soft butter
1 cup granulated sugar
4 eggs
1 (16-ounce) can chocolate-flavored syrup
1 1/4 cups all-purpose flour
1 cup chopped pecans
Confectioners' sugar, for dusting top

Super easy to make with no clean-up. Crispy on the outside, fudgy in the center.

Preheat oven to 350 degrees. Butter and flour, or spray with baking spray, a 9 x 13 x 2-inch baking pan. In large mixer bowl, cream together butter and sugar, mixing well. Add eggs and beat until thoroughly combined. Stir in pecans and pour into prepared pan. Bake 35 minutes. Remove pan from oven and place on rack to cool. When cool, cut into squares and sprinkle top with confectioners' sugar.
Yield: 1 dozen brownies

PUFFY PANCAKE FOR PAPA

"Some kids like to put maple syrup on top of their puffy pancake but not Papa! He likes fresh strawberries and kiwi fruit."

Though originally grown only in New Zealand, Islanders now enjoy Kiwi fruit grown right in our back yards, just across the Sound.

3 tablespoons butter
4 eggs
1/2 cup milk
1/8 teaspoon salt
1/2 cup all-purpose flour
Slices of fresh strawberries and kiwi for topping
Powdered sugar for dusting

Wash your hands very well. Preheat oven to 425 degrees. Put butter into 10-inch pie plate. Place in oven and leave just until butter is melted, then remove. Set aside. In medium bowl, mix together eggs and milk. Then add salt and flour and beat with an egg beater until smooth. Stir in melted butter from pie plate; mix well. Pour it all back into pie plate.

Put pie plate into oven and bake pancake 25 minutes until it is puffy and golden brown. Have Mom help you take it out of oven and top pancake with sliced strawberries and kiwi. Sprinkle with powdered sugar and cut into 4 wedges.
Yield: 4 servings

MRS. CLAUS' CHRISTMAS TREE
DESSERT PIZZA

1 (18-ounce) roll refrigerated sugar cookie dough
3 (3.5-ounce) containers refrigerated vanilla pudding
1 cup plain yogurt
4 to 6 kiwis, peeled and sliced into rounds
1 pint small-sized fresh strawberries, sliced into rounds
Dusting of red and green sugar sprinkles for decoration

Preheat oven to 350 degrees. Using your fingers, press cookie dough evenly into ungreased 12-inch pizza pan. Place in oven and bake 12 to 15 minutes, or until cookie dough is golden. Turn off oven. Remove pan from oven with hot mitts and place on cooling rack.

Put pudding and yogurt in a bowl and mix well. Using rubber spatula, spread mixture evenly over cooled cookie crust.

To decorate: Make a Christmas tree shape in center of dessert pizza by overlapping green kiwi slices. Use small strawberry rounds to make ornaments on tree, and use larger strawberry rounds to form a circle around edge of dessert pizza. Sprinkle remaining exposed pudding surface lightly with red and green sugar sprinkles.
Yield: 8 servings

You can have your cake and pudding too with this sweet dessert pizza! We're told Santa enjoys this when he gets back from his rounds on Christmas night.

WINTER CRISP

... the best way to eat oatmeal outside of Scotland.

3 red (MacIntosh or Rome) cooking apples

2 ripe pears

1 cup fresh cranberries, cut in half

2 to 4 tablespoons granulated sugar

1 to 2 teaspoons lemon juice

1 teaspoon cinnamon

Topping

3/4 cup all-purpose flour

3/4 cup rolled oats

3/4 cup brown sugar

9 tablespoons butter, softened

1/2 teaspoon cinnamon

Preheat oven to 375 degrees. Wash your hands. Grease, or spray with baking spray, an 8-inch square baking pan. Peel, core, and slice apples and pears into a bowl. Add cranberries. Add sugar, lemon juice, and cinnamon to fruits and toss together. Add extra sugar or lemon juice if it seems necessary. Spoon mixture into baking pan.

Combine topping ingredients: flour, rolled oats, brown sugar, butter, and cinnamon. Mix together with your hands and spread evenly over fruit.

Bake 30 to 40 minutes or until topping is golden brown. Cool at least 10 minutes. Then serve with frozen yogurt or ice cream.

Yield: 6 servings

JULIE'S MAGIC MACAROONS

4 egg whites
Pinch of salt
3/4 cup granulated sugar
1 teaspoon vanilla extract
2 cups shredded coconut

Preheat oven to 300 degrees. Lightly coat baking sheets with nonstick baking spray. Beat egg whites and salt with electric beaters until foamy. Gradually add sugar and vanilla, beating constantly until stiff (but not dry) peaks form. Stir in coconut. Drop batter onto prepared baking sheets by teaspoons. Bake about 15 minutes or until lightly browned. Store in airtight container.
Yield: 5 1/2 dozen macaroons

Bakers choice: you can make these Macaroons larger to use as a base for ice cream topped with strawberry sauce. Or, you can shape them with rims to make cups to hold fruit fillings.

HONEY PEANUT
BUTTER BUTTONS

1/2 cup honey
3/4 cup dry milk powder
1/2 cup peanut butter
1/2 cup chopped roasted peanuts

Mix together honey, milk powder, and peanut butter. With a teaspoon, scoop up small amounts of mixture. Roll between palms of hands to make small balls. Roll each ball in chopped peanuts and place on tray lined with wax paper. Press with thumb to flatten into button shapes. Refrigerate until needed.
Yield: 2 dozen cookies

An ideal no-bake cookie to make on a rainy day when Mom doesn't want to go to the store… supplies can usually be found right in the kitchen!

WINDOW PANE
SUGAR COOKIES

Candy melts during baking, making pretty cookies that look like stained glass.

2 cups all-purpose flour

1 1/2 teaspoons baking powder

1/4 teaspoon salt

6 tablespoons butter at room temperature

1/3 cup vegetable shortening

3/4 cup granulated sugar

1 tablespoon milk

1 egg

5 rolls of assorted flavor Life-savers, crushed

Sift together flour, baking powder, and salt. Set aside. In large mixer bowl, cream together butter and shortening until smooth. Add sugar and beat until fluffy. Add milk and egg; beat well. Blend in flour mixture to make stiff dough. Divide dough in half and chill 3 hours or overnight.

Preheat oven to 375 degrees. Line baking pans with parchment or aluminum foil. Roll out chilled dough to thickness of 1/8-inch. Cut into desired shapes with floured cookie cutters. Transfer to prepared baking pans. Cut small rounds from centers of each cookie with mini-cutter or pastry tube tip. Fill holes with crushed candy. Bake 7 to 8 minutes. Carefully remove cookies from parchment to cooling racks.
Yield: 3 1/2 dozen cookies

Cook's Note: If using Window Pane Sugar Cookies for Christmas tree ornaments, make a hole in each cookie, (with tip of skewer) prior to baking, so that string or twine may be inserted later for tying to tree.

TIGER BUTTER

... Grrrreat!

1 cup melted white chocolate (premium white
chocolate squares)
1/2 cup peanut butter, creamy or chunky
1/2 cup melted milk chocolate

Thoroughly mix white chocolate and peanut butter
together. Pour mixture on wax paper. Spoon melted
milk chocolate over peanut butter mixture. Draw a
spatula through it in a swirling motion to make a
marbleized pattern. Put into freezer to set. Cut into
small squares.
Yield: Lots more than Mom lets you eat at one time.

S'MORE CLUSTERS

A Christmas treat with
memories of summer
evenings by the campfire.

6 (1 1/2-ounce) milk chocolate candy bars
2 cups miniature marshmallows
2 1/2 cups coarsely chopped graham crackers

Microwave chocolate in medium microwaveable bowl
(don't ever use a metal bowl) for 1 minute. Stir.
Continue microwaving for 1 minute more and stir
until smooth.

Add marshmallows and chopped graham wafers,
stirring until coated with melted chocolate.

Spoon into decorative miniature cup cake liners. Lick
your fingers. Refrigerate until firm.
Yield: 12 clusters

COOKIE CLOUDS

Lots of great fun for kids!

This dessert is loaded

with goodies.

1 (8-ounce) carton frozen whipped topping, thawed
12 packaged chocolate chip cookies
1/2 cup milk
Toppings
Hot fudge sauce
Chopped pecans
Maraschino cherries

Place a dollop of whipped topping into each of four dessert glasses. Dip each cookie quickly into milk and place on top of whipped topping. Repeat layers of topping and cookies ending with whipped topping. Cover and chill at least 2 hours. Add toppings, as desired, to each serving.
Yield: 4 servings

BERRIES-IN-THE-SNOW

More fun for the kids .

With a little patience

they can also make

a snowman.

6 premium white chocolate baking squares
3/4 cup dried cranberries

Unwrap baking squares and place in a microwavable bowl. Microwave on High for 2 to 2 1/2 minutes. Stir half-way through heating time. The squares will retain some of their original shapes; remove from microwave and stir until smooth. If not completely smooth return to microwave for 10 seconds, one or more times. When smooth stir in dried cranberries. With two teaspoons, scoop mixture onto a sheet of wax paper, making clusters about the size of a half dollar. When set, store in covered container.
Yield: 12 to 14 clusters

JANE'S PEPPERMINT CRUNCH ICE-CREAM PIE

The Pie Shell
6 ounces semisweet chocolate chips
2 tablespoons butter
2 cups rice cereal
1/2 cup chopped walnuts

Butter 9 inch pie plate. Melt chocolate chips and butter in saucepan over low heat, stirring until smooth. Remove from heat; mix in cereal and nuts. Press mixture into pie plate covering bottom and sides. Set aside until needed.

The Ice Cream
1 quart best quality vanilla ice cream
1/2 cup coarsely crushed peppermint candy canes
1/2 cup finely crushed peppermint candy canes
Purchased Chocolate Sauce

Soften ice cream slightly in carton and scoop into a bowl. Stir crushed candy canes into ice cream until well blended. Spoon ice cream back into carton and place in freezer until needed. At serving time, pack ice cream into Pie Shell and drizzle with Chocolate Sauce.

Chocolate Sauce
6 ounces semisweet chocolate chips
1/3 cup milk
2 tablespoons butter

Combine chocolate chips, milk and butter in small saucepan. Heat slowly, stirring constantly until smooth. Cool.
Yield: 6 servings

Instead of making a pie, sometimes you might like to serve the ice cream with just a Chocolate Sauce that you buy.
If you'd like to make Chocolate Sauce from scratch, try the recipe included.

SOFT PRETZELS

2 packages active dry yeast
1 1/2 cups warm water
2 tablespoons sugar
1 teaspoon salt
4 cups all-purpose flour
1 egg, beaten
Sprinkling of coarse salt

In a large mixing bowl combine yeast and water. Add sugar and salt. Stir in flour until fully combined. Cover and allow dough to rise for 20 minutes. Scoop dough onto floured surface (the counter will be fine) and begin to knead.

To knead, place both hands on dough, and push away from yourself with the heels of your hands. You may ask Mom to help until you get the hang of it.

Once dough is no longer sticky, cut it into about 36 pieces of equal size.

Roll each piece on floured surface to resemble a 12-inch long pencil. Then pick up pencil-shaped dough by each end and cross over to form rabbit ears. Twist ends at point of cross over and pull back to rest on loop.

Preheat oven to 425 degrees. Brush pretzels with beaten egg. Sprinkle with coarse salt. Bake for 10 to 15 minutes, until puffed and golden. Eat!
Yield: 36 pretzels

POPCORN BALL TREATS

2 cups granulated sugar
1/2 cup light corn syrup
1/2 cup water
2 tablespoons butter
1 tablespoon vinegar
1 tablespoon vanilla extract
3/4 teaspoon salt
10 quarts popcorn, unsalted and unbuttered

Place sugar, corn syrup and water in saucepan. Bring to boil, reduce heat and cook to soft ball stage (your Mom will help you here). Remove from heat and stir in butter, vinegar, vanilla, and salt.

Oil a great big bowl. Place about 6 quarts of the popcorn into it. With wooden spoon, stir popcorn while pouring the hot sugar syrup over. Continuing to stir, add as much additional popcorn as can be incorporated.

With your Mom or a friend helping, butter your hands and quickly form popcorn into 2-inch balls. Place them on wax paper as they are formed. Cover with wax paper and a towel to dry overnight. Next day, store in air-tight containers.
Yield: 4 dozen popcorn balls

Cook's Note: Working quickly, you can also pack the popcorn into sprayed plastic animal molds.

"When growing up in Wisconsin, my German Grandmother arrived each Christmas day bearing gifts and a huge tin the size of a hatbox, containing at least 100 of these popcorn balls."

ENDURING YULETIDE TRADITIONS

On Hilton Head the mild comfortable days and evenings of November and December make it a little difficult to get into the holiday spirit ... until those first Thanksgiving hayrides begin through the Sea Pines Forest Preserve. If the wagons are full, there is another chance at Christmas time to go caroling on the same route.

The week before Thanksgiving we all tuck ourselves into the dream of dancing nutcrackers and sugar plum fairies as the Hilton Head Dance Theater presents its annual version of 'The Nutcracker' at the Self Family Arts Center.

The 'Festival of Trees' is a seasonal joy that puts stars in the eyes of the entire family as they wander through a maze of individually decorated Christmas trees ... all sizes, some quite sophisticated, some whimsical, and all can be bagged to take home.

The popular 'Gingerbread Village' features art-in-the-oven-original, edible creations from amateur and professional chefs. Just the thought of ginger-bread brings a smile to the faces of everyone but the most stiff-necked Scrooge.

Outstanding holiday-musicals are performed each Yuletide at the Elizabeth Wallace Theater ...from the world premier of 'The Christmas Carol', adapted by award-winning novelist, Islander John Jakes, to the youthful adaptation of O'Henry's 'Gift of the Magi.'

Heartwarming holiday-inspired music is heard throughout the festive season. The Hilton Head Orchestra Concert Series presents their special Holiday Concert, one of ten concerts each year. The Hilton Head Choral Society thrills its audience with the 'Messiah' and the 'Christmas Cantata'.

Yuletide celebrates 'Christmas Through the Ages' with carols from The Hallelujah Singers, poetry readings, orchestral presentations and The Night Before Christmas in Gullah.

There is a live nativity at Lawton Stables on Christmas Eve.

While we won't trudge through snow to Grandma's house on Christmas morning – a brisk walk on the beach will make us thankful for the wonderful Island we call home.

HE SPIRIT OF GIVING

Holiday food gifts

are not an option on Hilton Head Island.

We believe that Yuletide is a time

for giving

sumptuous goodies to family, friends, and neighbors

as the best expression of caring.

You can be sure your guests will arrive

at your door with

a festively wrapped specialty of their own making.

Islanders believe it is blessèd

to give and to receive

...

everybody does it.

HOT FUDGE PEPPERMINT STICK SAUCE

2/3 cup heavy cream
2 tablespoons unsalted butter, cut into pieces
1/2 cup packed light brown sugar
2-ounces finely chopped unsweetened chocolate
1/8 teaspoon salt
1/2 cup coarsely crushed peppermint-stick candy

Combine cream and butter in heavy saucepan and bring to boil. Lower heat, add brown sugar, and whisk until dissolved. Add chocolate and salt. Continue whisking while simmering until chocolate has melted and become smooth. Stir in peppermint candy and remove from heat. Pour into sterilized jars and seal. Serve warm over ice cream.
Yield: 2 half-pint jars

For a nice gift presentation, picture colorful red and green ribbons tied at the rim of the jar with a miniature candy cane and sprig of holly.

BUTTERSCOTCH RUM SAUCE

1 cup firmly light brown sugar
1/4 cup light corn syrup
1/2 stick unsalted butter
Pinch of salt
1/2 cup heavy cream
1 1/2 teaspoons vanilla
1/4 teaspoon fresh lemon juice
1 1/2 tablespoons dark rum, or to taste
1/2 cup coarsely chopped toasted pecans

In a small heavy saucepan combine brown sugar, corn syrup, butter and a pinch of salt. Cook mixture over moderate heat, stirring until sugar is dissolved. Wash down any sugar crystals clinging to side of pan with a brush dipped in cold water. Boil, undisturbed, to 238 degrees. Remove from heat and stir in remaining ingredients. Pour into 2 half-pint sterilized jars and seal tightly. Refrigerate until needed or until given as a gift.
Yield: 2 half-pint jars

A sumptuous sauce that sets apart anything you serve.

BLUFFTON
ARTICHOKE RELISH

This tart and crunchy

relish made with

Jerusalem Artichokes is

so-o-o-o Lowcountry.

These roots of native

American sunflowers are

often referred to as

sunchokes. Knobby and

irregularly shaped, they

grow wild in the South,

and in our backyards.

This relish is a best-seller

at the Bluffton

Church of the Cross

Christmas Bazaar

each year. They use their

washing machines to

clean the chokes.

1 cup coarse kosher salt
4 quarts water
2 pounds Jerusalem artichokes, scrubbed well, chopped
2 cups chopped Vidalia onions
1 red bell pepper, seeded, chopped
1 green bell pepper, seeded, chopped
3 tablespoons dry mustard
1 tablespoon ground turmeric
1/8 teaspoon cayenne pepper
2 cups sugar
1 quart cider vinegar

Mix salt and water in a large ceramic or stainless steel bowl. Add chopped artichokes, peppers and onions. Cover and refrigerate 24 hours.

Next day, drain, squeezing out all excess moisture. Sprinkle mustard, turmeric and cayenne over vegetables and mix thoroughly. In nonreactive pot, dissolve sugar in vinegar, bring to boil, and pour over artichoke mixture.

Fill sterilized jars, seal, and process in boiling water bath for 15 minutes. Age for a week or more before using. Store in pantry for months and in refrigerator indefinitely.
Yield: 5 pints

TRIPLE CITRUS MARMALADE

1 large thin skinned pink grapefruit
1 thin-skinned orange
2 large tangerines
5 cups water
1 1/2 cups sugar

Using vegetable peeler, remove colored part of peel
from grapefruit, orange and tangerines. Chop peel
coarsely. Bring 4 cups water to boil in saucepan. Add
peel and boil 10 minutes. Drain peel, rinse under cold
water, and drain again. Cut away all pith from fruits.
Cut fruits into 1/2-inch pieces, discarding seeds and
reserving any fruit juices.

Combine chopped peel, chopped fruit, reserved
juices, sugar and remaining 1 cup water in heavy
large saucepan. Stir mixture over medium heat until
sugar dissolves. Increase heat and boil marmalade,
uncovered, stirring frequently until very thick and jell
point is reached, or until 1 tablespoon of juice jells
when refrigerated for 3 minutes. Begin testing after 40
minutes. Spoon hot marmalade into hot clean jars.
Cool. Store in refrigerator.
Yield: 2 half-pints

This pretty amber colored marmalade combines the sweet-tart juices and peels of three citrus fruits: grapefruit, orange, and tangerine. Delicious when spread on Angel Biscuits with Country Ham.

GOLDEN APPLE CHUTNEY

A raffia ribbon tied around the jar with two or three dried apple slices tied into the bow makes a delicious condiment an even more festive gift.

8 to 10 Golden Delicious apples, peeled, cored and diced
1 cup finely chopped pecans
2 cups golden raisins
Zest from 2 navel oranges, finely chopped
4 cups granulated sugar
1/2 cup apple cider vinegar
1/3 teaspoon ground cloves

Place all ingredients in non-reactive saucepan over moderately high heat.

Bring to boil, lower heat and simmer, stirring constantly, about 15 minutes, or until apples and pecans are tender. Spoon into sterilized jars and seal tightly. Refrigerate after opening.
Yield: 6 half-pint jars

CRISPY SPICED PECANS

Fill interesting glass boxes or very simple jars with these crunchy pecans. To serve as a knob on container, glue a whole unshelled pecan on the lid.

1 egg white
1 tablespoon cold water
1 pound pecan halves
1/2 cup granulated sugar
1/4 teaspoon salt
1/2 teaspoon ground cinnamon
1/2 teaspoon ground cloves

Preheat oven to 225 degrees. Beat egg white and water together until frothy. Mix in pecans. Combine sugar, salt, and spices. Coat pecans evenly with sugar mixture. Place on cookie sheet. Bake at 225 degrees 1 hour, turning every 15 minutes.
Yield: 3 cups

CHRISTMAS MINTS

1/2 cup unsalted butter
1-pound confectioners' sugar
3 tablespoons warm water
2 teaspoons peppermint extract
Red and green food coloring

Make these melt-in-your-mouth mints as an after dinner sweet or as a special gift for a friend's holiday tea table.

Cream butter and sugar together; add water and peppermint and mix well. Divide mixture into three portions. Leave one portion white; add red and green food coloring to each of the remaining two portions until desired color is reached.

Prepare one sheet parchment paper for each color. Using 3/4-inch cookie cutter, or small jar, trace (with a pencil) 30 circles on each of two sheets of parchment paper and 20 circles on one. Turn paper over (rings will show through). Spoon each color of mint mixture into a separate pastry bag with small tip. Pipe white and red mint mixtures onto parchment sheets with 30 circles. Pipe green mints onto parchment with 20 circles.

With remaining mint mixture in white pastry bag, add a small white dot to each of the red and green mints. With remaining mixture in green pastry bag, pipe a small green dot onto the white mints. Change tip on green pastry bag to leaf tip. To the side of the dots on red and green mints, add a small leaf. Allow mints to stand 24 hours to dry thoroughly. Place in petit four cups for packaging.
Yield: 30 red and white mints, 20 green mints

BON BON COOKIES

C'est Si Bon ~

Bon Bons!

Arrange these colorful

cookies on a Christmas

plate (which could

actually be part

of the gift.)

1 cup vegetable shortening
1 1/2 cups confectioners' sugar
1 egg, beaten
1/2 teaspoon vanilla extract
1/2 teaspoon almond extract
2 1/4 cups sifted all-purpose flour
1/2 teaspoon soda
1/2 teaspoon cream of tartar
1/2 teaspoon salt
Red, green, and yellow food coloring
Whole blanched almonds, split in halves

Preheat oven to 350 degrees. Cream shortening and sugar; add egg, vanilla and almond extracts. Beat until light and lemon in color. Sift together flour, soda, cream of tartar and salt; beat into creamed ingredients.

Divide dough into four parts. Leave one part white; add red, green, and yellow food coloring to each of the remaining three parts. Form into 1-inch balls and place on parchment lined baking sheet. Dip bottom of glass in flour and flatten each ball. Place almond on each cookie.

Bake 8 minutes, watching to make sure cookies do not brown. Pull parchment paper containing cookies onto cooling rack. Cool and store, or package for gift giving.
Yield: 4 dozen cookies

VISIONS OF SUGAR PLUMS

1 cup dried apricots
1 cup pecan halves
1/2 cup pitted dates
1/2 cup golden raisins
1 cup vanilla wafer crumbs
1 cup flaked coconut
1/2 cup orange juice
1/2 cup granulated sugar

Place apricots, pecans, dates, raisins and wafer crumbs in bowl of food processor. Process until finely chopped and beginning to stick together. Transfer to mixing bowl. Add coconut and orange juice; stir to combine. With hands form into 1-inch balls. Roll in granulated sugar, and place each in paper candy cup, or wrap in squares of clear cellophane, twist at top, and tie with ribbon.
Yield: 3 dozen sugar plums

Modern-day sugar plums don't exactly dance in your head, but we think they may just do a little pirouette, with your taste buds.

JAMAICAN RUM BALLS

1 box (3 packets) cinnamon graham crackers
1 (14-ounce) package flaked coconut
2 cups chopped pecans
1 (14-ounce) can sweetened condensed milk
1/3 cup dark Jamaican rum
Confectioners' sugar

Crush graham crackers in plastic bag or food processor to make fine crumbs. Add coconut and pecans; toss to combine. Stir condensed milk and rum together. Pour over crumb mixture, and stir until ingredients are well combined. Allow to stand, lightly covered, for about 4 hours. Form into 1-inch balls and roll in confectioners' sugar until well coated.
Yield: 4 dozen rum balls

Place rum balls in holiday-imprinted petit four cups and arrange in small brass or silver gift boxes for giving.

Cook's Note: Store in one layer, or with wax paper between layers.

SPICED PECAN CLUSTERS

... a close cousin

to Pralines and so

easy to make.

3 pounds pecan halves
2 cups granulated sugar
1 cup water
1 tablespoon ground cinnamon
1 tablespoon ground allspice
1 tablespoon ground ginger
1 tablespoon ground nutmeg
1 teaspoon salt

Place pecans in a shallow baking pan, and toast in a 350 degree oven for 15 minutes, stirring once or twice. Combine all remaining ingredients in a saucepan and cook, without stirring, over moderately high heat until soft ball stage, or until 238 degrees is reached on candy thermometer. Pour over pecans. Stir gently until creamy and sugary taking care not to break the nuts. Drop by spoonsful onto wax paper forming small clusters. When cool, wrap clusters individually in plastic wrap.
Yield: 8 (8-ounce) gift containers

SUSAN'S CAROB TRUFFLES

A nutritious, healthy,

and quite different

take-off on a classic

confection. Ingredients

can be found in most

health food stores.

1/2 cup carob powder
1/2 cup sunflower seeds
1/2 cup sesame seeds
1/2 cup wheat germ
1/2 cup honey
1/2 cup peanut butter
Grated coconut

Mix together first 4 ingredients. Add honey and peanut butter and stir until well blended. Mixture will be very firm. Roll into balls. Roll in coconut to coat evenly. If desired, place each truffle in miniature paper cup. Store in refrigerator until ready to package for gifts.
Yield: 3 dozen truffles

CHOCOLATE TRUFFLES
GRAND MARNIER

8 ounces high quality semisweet chocolate
1/3 cup heavy cream
1 tablespoon Grand Marnier
1/4 cup cocoa powder, sifted

Chop chocolate into small pieces. In a heavy saucepan, heat cream to boiling. Remove from heat, add chocolate and stir until moistened evenly. Cover; let stand 5 minutes. Stir gently until chocolate is melted. Stir in Grand Marnier. Beat chocolate until cool and color has lightened. Mixture will thicken and appear rough, which is all right.

Spoon portion the size of large marble into palm of hand. Roll between the palms to form a ball and drop each into sifted cocoa. Roll to cover completely. Transfer to paper truffle cups. Refrigerate until ready to package for gift giving. Refrigerate packaged truffles until delivered.
Yield: 2 dozen decadent truffles

How can anything this good be so easy to make? You can cross many names off your gift list in just one candy-making session.

Eggnog and rum add an addictive depth and rich taste to this velvety white chocolate fudge.

WHITE CHOCOLATE EGGNOG FUDGE

2 cups granulated sugar
1/2 cup butter
3/4 cup dairy eggnog
3 (3 1/2-ounce) white chocolate candy bars, broken into pieces
1/2 teaspoon freshly grated nutmeg
1 (7-ounce) jar marshmallow creme
1 cup chopped pecans
1 teaspoon rum extract

Combine sugar, butter and eggnog in heavy 3-quart saucepan; bring to rolling boil, stirring constantly. Continue boiling and stirring 8 to 10 minutes, or until candy thermometer reaches 234 degrees.

Remove from heat; stir in white chocolate and nutmeg. When chocolate has melted stir in marshmallow creme, nuts and rum extract. Beat until well blended. Pour into buttered 9-inch square pan. Cool to room temperature. Cut into squares.
Yield: 72 squares

DARCY'S CHOCOLATE MARSHMALLOW FUDGE

2 tablespoons butter
2/3 cup evaporated milk
1 1/2 cup granulated sugar
1/4 teaspoon salt
1 teaspoon vanilla extract
12 ounces semisweet chocolate chips
2 cups mini-marshmallows

Combine butter, milk, sugar, salt and vanilla in saucepan. Heat to boiling. Reduce heat to medium and stir for 5 minutes. Stir in chocolate and marshmallows until melted and well combined.

Butter an 8-inch square pan. Pour in fudge and spread evenly. Refrigerate until firm. Cut into 1-inch squares.
Yield: 4 dozen squares

... the quintessential chocolate fudge ... perhaps the first you learned to master, and have never ceased to crave.

WALNUT PENUCHE

1 cup granulated sugar
1 cup packed light brown sugar
1 cup light cream
1 tablespoon dark rum
2 cups broken walnuts

Combine sugars and cream in heavy saucepan; bring to boil, stirring constantly. Wash down any sugar crystals forming on sides of pan with brush dipped in cold water. Reduce heat; simmer undisturbed until thermometer registers 238 degrees. Remove from heat and cool 5 minutes.

Add rum and beat until thickened. Meanwhile lay walnuts in bottom of buttered 8-inch square pan. Pour candy mixture over walnuts. Tilt pan until candy mixture is spread evenly. Cool completely and cut into 1-inch squares. Store in airtight tins lined with wax paper. Place wax paper between layers. Can be made 2 weeks ahead.
Yield: 64 (1-inch) squares

… and this is the real old-fashioned walnut fudge remembered from childhood.

OLD MISSOURI POUND CAKE

A taste of American heritage is captured in this butter-enriched pound cake. It is guaranteed to become an oft-repeated recipe.

8 eggs, separated

1/3 cup granulated sugar

1 pound butter at room temperature

2 1/3 cups granulated sugar

1 teaspoon lemon extract

3 1/2 cups all-purpose flour, sifted

1/2 cup half and half

Preheat oven to 325 degrees. Butter and flour, or spray with bakers' spray, two 9 x 5-inch loaf pans. With electric mixer, beat egg whites until foamy. Gradually add 1/3 cup sugar, beating until firm peaks have formed.

In another large mixer bowl, cream together butter, 2 1/3 cups sugar, egg yolks and lemon extract. With mixer at low speed, add flour and cream alternately. Fold in beaten egg whites by hand. Spoon batter into prepared loaf pans.

Bake 1 hour and 45 minutes or until top springs back when touched. Test after 90 minutes. Cool a few minutes. Remove from pan and finish cooling on rack. Wrap in plastic and tie with Christmas ribbons when giving as a gift.

Yield: 2 loaves

WHIPPED CREAM POUND CAKE

1/2 pound butter, at room temperature
3 cups granulated sugar
6 eggs
1 cup whipping cream, lightly whipped
3 cups sifted all-purpose flour
2 teaspoons vanilla extract

Cream butter and sugar together. Add eggs, one at a time, beating well after each addition. Beat in cream and flour alternately to form a well blended batter.

Spoon into buttered and floured 10-inch bundt pan. Place in cold oven, turn to 325 degrees and bake for 1 1/2 hours or until toothpick inserted in cake comes out clean.
Yield: 12 servings

May also be baked in miniature loaf pans for Christmas giving. Add a tag saying it's very good when sliced and toasted for breakfast.

MINI BUTTER RUM POUND CAKES

...a good way

to delight

six good friends.

1 cup butter, softened
2 1/2 cups granulated sugar
6 egg yolks
3 cups all-purpose flour
1/4 teaspoon baking soda
1 cup sour cream
1 teaspoon each vanilla and lemon extract
6 egg whites
1/2 cup granulated sugar

Preheat oven to 325 degrees. Spray 6 mini-bundt pans with baker's spray.

In large mixer bowl, cream together butter, sugar and egg yolks. Sift together flour and soda; add to creamed mixture alternately with sour cream, beginning and ending with flour. Stir in vanilla and lemon extracts.

Beat egg whites, gradually adding 1/2 cup sugar until firm peaks have formed; gently fold into batter. Spoon into mini-bundt pans. Bake 40 to 50 minutes or until cakes test done (wooden pick when inserted, comes out clean).

Cool briefly in pans; remove to cooling racks. Perforate cakes in several places with skewer. While still warm, spoon Buttered Rum Glaze over cakes.

Buttered Rum Glaze
6 tablespoons butter
1/2 cup chopped sliced almonds
3 tablespoons water
4 tablespoons dark rum
3/4 cup light brown sugar

Melt butter in saucepan; add almonds and sauté until golden. Add water, rum and brown sugar all at once. Stir until sugar has melted.

Yield: 6 mini-bundt cakes

FRUIT & LEMON NUT CAKE

1 cup all-purpose flour, for dredging
1 pound pecan halves
1 pound glacé red cherries
1 pound golden raisins
1 tablespoon grated lemon rind
1 pound butter, melted and cooled
1 pound granulated sugar
6 eggs
3 cups all-purpose flour
1 teaspoon each baking powder and salt
1 teaspoon lemon extract (or more for greater lemon flavor)
1 teaspoon vanilla extract

... a tangy lemon flavor is appealing any time. As a year-round gift you can bake this lemon and nut cake without the glacé cherries.

Preheat oven to 300 degrees. Grease and lightly flour or spray a 10-inch tube pan. Dredge nuts, cherries, raisins, and lemon rind in 1 cup of flour. Set aside.

Place butter in large mixer bowl. Beat in sugar gradually and add eggs one at a time, beating well after each addition

Sift together flour, baking powder and salt. Beat into creamed mixture. Add lemon and vanilla extracts. Spoon into baking pan. Bake 2 hours or until toothpick inserted in center, comes out clean. Turn out onto rack to cool. Wrap well and store in cool place

This cake keeps well and is best served at room temperature. Slice thinly to serve.
Yield: 16 servings

HEAVENLY HAZELNUT CAKE

…not time consuming

but certainly gives

that impression.

Hazelnuts, so popular in

Europe, are growing in

favor here, thanks to the

fine quality of our

Oregon harvest.

8 eggs, separated
1 cup granulated sugar, divided
1 teaspoon vanilla extract
1/2 pound ground hazelnuts
1 tablespoon cornstarch
1/2 teaspoon instant coffee granules
1 1/2 teaspoons baking powder

Preheat oven to 350 degrees. Line 10-inch springform pan with parchment and spray with baking spray. In large mixer bowl, beat egg whites until foamy. Gradually beat in 1/2 cup of sugar until very firm peaks form. Set aside.

Beat egg yolks, remaining 1/2 cup sugar and vanilla together until light and lemon colored. Combine hazelnuts, cornstarch, coffee granules and baking powder; fold into yolk mixture. Fold beaten egg whites into hazelnut mixture. Spoon into prepared springform pan. Bake 60 to 70 minutes. Cool slightly, release sides of springform pan and transfer to rack to finish cooling. Wrap as gift, or store in covered container until needed.
Yield: 12 servings

HUNGARIAN CHRISTMAS FRUITCAKE

An irresistible moist Christmas cake ... an experience to make and a joy to give!

Mini-Loaf Pan Preparation
1/2 cup butter, melted
2 cups brown sugar
1/4 cup apricot brandy
1/2 pound dried pitted prunes, cooked
1/2 pound dried apricot halves, cooked
1/2 cup pecan halves

Note that the cakes will be turned upside-down for presentation. Butter 8 mini-loaf pans. Stir together melted butter, brown sugar and brandy. Divide among the pans and spread to cover bottoms evenly. Arrange cooked prunes, apricots, and pecan halves (upside-down) on brown sugar base in each pan.

The Fruitcake
1 cup vegetable shortening
2 1/2 cups brown sugar
4 eggs, beaten
3 1/2 cups all-purpose flour
1/2 teaspoon each ginger, allspice and cloves
1 teaspoon each cinnamon and nutmeg
1 teaspoon each salt and baking soda
1/2 cup apricot brandy
1 cup each prune juice and apricot juice
1 1/2 cups each chopped prunes and dried apricots
2 cups chopped pecans, tossed with 1/2 cup flour

Preheat oven to 300 degrees. Cream together shortening, brown sugar and eggs. Sift together flour, spices, salt and soda. Beat into creamed mixture alternately with liquid ingredients (brandy and fruit juices). Fold in chopped prunes, apricots, and pecans. Divide batter evenly among prepared mini-loaf pans.

Bake 1 hour or until tooth pick inserted in center of cakes comes out clean. Cool about 3 minutes; turn out of pans to finish cooling on rack. Wrap in plastic, to reveal design, for Christmas giving.
Yield: 8 mini-fruitcakes

A SPECIAL WAY OF LIFE

Whether you're a permanent Islander, a part-timer, or a visitor just discovering the bounty of Hilton Head, you know there is something special about the Island.

It's the people!

From the moment of arrival... crossing the arc of the bridge... flying over waterways to arrive at our airport... navigating the Intracoastal to dock in an Island harbor – there is an immediate sense of being removed from the rest of the world.

People from all walks of life have come here creating a stimulating environment. Many came just to "look" and have stayed because of the quality of life. It's more than a community... it's also a hometown... a hometown of people caring about, and sharing with, one another.

It's the people who have made it this way!

Virtually unknown to the rest of the world in 1957, Hilton Head is now known world-wide as one of the finest South Atlantic coast resorts and residences in the country.

Apart from the frenetic pace from which most of us came, Hilton Head is instead an enchanting haven where the tempo of life beats in harmony with nature. Where Islanders enjoy miles of winding bicycle and walking trails... where the splendor of the sea, sky, and maritime forest all blend seamlessly with the luxuries of a world-class resort.

The people have kept it this way!

This is a place where culture and the arts thrive as effortlessly as the marsh side's snowy egret or as dolphins enjoying the nearness of the shoreline and proximity of a shrimp boat's wake.

The people have made it happen this way!

Life on Hilton Head continues as an affirmation of the Island's capacity to delight, surprise and provide. We are the melting pot of a young American community developed in only 30 years.

Life here is good, as good as it can get any place on earth, because of the Island's history, its seaside magic, and its lyrical beauty. And yes, the people – it's unquestionably the people!

VERY MERRY MENUS
A MONTAGE OF ISLAND FAVORITES

The editors have created these menus for entertaining from our eclectic Yuletide collection. They reflect what we would typically prepare on Hilton Head for those festive occasions when we're proudest of our marvelous 'Heritage of Island Flavors.'

THANKSGIVING
ON THE SOUND

Escargots in Edible Mushroom Shells   p23

Wonderfully Simple Roast Turkey   p75
Calibogue Oyster Stuffing   p114
Lowcountry Sweet Potatoes with Praline Topping   p109
Sprouts & Chestnuts   p104
Piquant Cranberry Conserve   p122
Mixed Green Salad

Pumpkin Amaretto Mousse with Whipped Cream   p142

Beringer Alluvium

HOT SPICED PORT

In a medium non-reactive saucepan, dissolve 1 teaspoon sugar in

2 teaspoons water over moderate heat. Add 2 cups port wine,

pinch each of ground cloves, ground allspice, and freshly

ground nutmeg. Warm over gentle heat about 5 minutes.

Pour into stemmed wine glasses. Serve with a strip

of lemon zest and a pinch of nutmeg. Serves 4

A WEEK-END
FAMILY GATHERING

Miz Maybelle's Turkey Bone Soup   p44

Ruby Cran-Raspberry Ring   p51
Gebhardt's Rhinelander Kohl Slaw   p51
Sea Island Muffins   p183

Ice Cream with Christmas Lace Cookies   p199

Pinot Gris / Pinot Grigio

CITRUS MINT REFRESHER

Heat 1 cup orange juice, 1/2 cup granulated sugar, and
12 sprigs fresh mint to boiling. Remove from heat and strain.
Stir in another cup of orange juice and 1/4 cup fresh
lime juice. Refrigerate syrup until needed.
To serve, pour 1/3 cup citrus syrup and 2/3 cup club soda
over ice cubes in tall glasses. Serves 6

WHEN ISLANDERS DO LUNCH

Asparagus Spears with White Cheese Dipping Sauce p27
Baked Rosemary Olives p29

Skull Creek Crab Cakes with
Roasted Red Pepper Coulis p19
Watercress, Apple, and Roquefort on Greens p153

Chocolate Mousse Cake p146

*Rosé from
Provence, France or Navarra, Spain*

TANGERINE ORANGE MIMOSA

Chill 1 bottle Champagne until very cold.

Squeeze 1 cup tangerine juice and 3 cups orange juice. Combine

and chill well. (Or, if available, use ready-prepared combination of

juices from Florida.) To serve, pour equal amounts of Champagne

and juice into chilled stemmed glasses. Garnish as desired. Serves 8

YULETIDE OPEN HOUSE

Boiled Carolina Shrimp on Ice with Remoulade Sauce p15
Daufuskie Spindled Oysters p20
Olde English Spiced Beef p32

Cheese and Almond Pinecones p26
Jeweled Cranberry Salad p125
Savory Pecans p28

Jane's Fruitcake Cookies p200
Christmas Lace Cookies p199
Bon Bon Cookies p142

Champagne Punch p269

SWEDISH GLÖGG

*Tie peel from an orange, 10 cardamom seeds, 10 cloves, 3 sticks
cinnamon and a small piece of fresh ginger in a 9-inch square of
cheesecloth. In large non-reactive saucepan or kettle, mix 1/2 cup
granulated sugar and 2 cups water. Add spice bag; bring to boil and
boil 10 minutes. Add 1 cup blanched almonds, 1 cup raisins, 6
coarsely chopped dried figs, 1 bottle (750 ml) brandy and 2 bottles
(750 ml) port. Heat but do not boil. Glögg is best made a few days in
advance and gently warmed just before serving. Serves 16*

DECK THE HALLS
FOR BRUNCH

Southern Ambrosia p115

Overnight Eggs Portuguese with Sausage p171
Christmas Spinach Salad p57
Apple Walnut Streusel p181

Cranberry Sorbet p133

Holly's Whipped Shortbread p196
Kentucky Bourbon Fruitcake p155

Asti Spumonti or Reisling

SPIRITED EGGNOG

Combine 3 quarts dairy eggnog, 3 1/3 cups rye, Scotch, or
bourbon, 1/2 cup Jamaican rum and 1/4 cup Cognac. Refrigerate
several hours or overnight. To serve, transfer to chilled punch bowl.
Whip 2 cups heavy cream to form soft peaks. Fold 1 cup into
eggnog. Place remaining whipped cream in a pretty bowl next to
punch bowl. Invite your guests to top individual servings with a
dollop of whipped cream and a sprinking of nutmeg. Serves 24

THE NUTCRACKER TEA TABLE

Buttermilk Currant Scones p186
Whipped Butter or Devon Cream
Cranberry Pear Chutney p122

Charleston Potted Shrimp on Bell-Shaped Toast Points p18

Whipped Cream Pound Cake p249
Pecan Macaroons p213
Lemon Kiss Surprise p197
Brandy Snaps p196

Coconut Mincemeat Bars p204
Hungarian Christmas Fruitcake p253

Selection of English Teas

NITA'S SPICED TEA

Tie 1 teaspoon each ground nutmeg and whole cloves, plus
stick of cinnamon in cheesecloth; place in non-reactive saucepan with
4 cups cold water. Boil, uncovered, 10 minutes. Tie 1/4 cup tea leaves
in cheesecloth and add to spice mixture along with 12 cups boiling
water. Remove from heat and allow to steep 5 minutes. Remove tea
bag, but leave spice bag. Add 1 cup each fresh orange and lemon juice.
Cool and refrigerate. May be served warm by reheating, or served cold
over ice cubes, as the occasion demands. Keeps well. Serves 25

DESSERT BUFFET
AFTER THE PERFORMANCE

Viennese Chestnut Torte Mit Schlag p145
Sherried Fresh Fruit Trifle p140
Chocolate Mousse Cake p146

Dottie Dunbar's Orange Cranberry Torte p150

Merry Mandlebrot p206
Noel Berry's Yuletide Cookies p208

Espresso Cups

Vin Santo, Ice Wine, or Australian Muscat

❦

IRISH COFFEE

Make your best pot of coffee a little on the strong side.

Have ready sugar cubes and whipping cream, well chilled. For each

cup, place one or two sugar cubes in bottom of cup and add a splash

of Irish Whiskey. Fill almost to top with hot coffee. Float whipping

cream on top. "Floating cream" can be accomplished by holding a

teaspoon upside down just over surface of coffee and gently pouring

cream over bowl of spoon. As an easy alternative, just whip

the cream and spoon it on top lightly.

page 262

CANDLELIGHT & CHAMPAGNE

Individual Oyster Soufflés p21

Roasted Rock Cornish Hens with Cumberland Sauce p71
Caramelized New Potatoes p106
Green Bean & Vidalia Onion Gratinée p103

Holiday Cranberry Pie à la Mode p129

Champagne (Brut, Blanc de Blanc)

KIR ROYALE

Chill a bottle of Champagne. Using a fine French Cassis or Chambord

pour 1/2 teaspoon Cassis into a tall crystal tulip glass.

Pour champagne slowly until half-full.

In the 20's, Père Kir, mayor of Dijon, France, first made this aperitif to

help increase champagne sales. It was named for him by his admirers.

Some have been known to toast the Mayor of Dijon, before toasting

the guest of honor, at parties where Kir Royale is served.

(Kir is made by substituting Chardonnay for Champagne.)

TRIM THE TREE PARTY

The Adams Family Christmas Tree p37
Watercress, Apple, and Roquefort on Greens p53

Boeuf Bourguignon Noël p87
Crusty French Bread

Vanilla Ice Cream with Hot Fudge Peppermint Stick Sauce p237
Scottish Shortbread p195
Michelle's One-Bowl Brownies p223

Cranberry Egg Nog p119
Old-Fashioned Mulled Wine p264

OLD-FASHIONED MULLED WINE

Combine 2 cups each water and sugar. Add an orange and

a lemon, thinly sliced. Add 2 cinnamon sticks and 12 each, cloves

and allspice berries. Bring to boil, lower heat and simmer 5 minutes.

Add 2 bottles dry red wine; simmer 10 minutes.

Serve in mugs with whole cinnamon sticks as stirrers. Serves 10

KIDS COOK WITH GRANDMA

Savory Christmas Wreath Pizza   p218
Celery and Carrot Sticks with Sweet Pickle Slices

Peppermint Crunch Ice Cream   p231
'Smore Clusters and Cookie Clouds   p229

Cranberry Egg Nog   p119

APPLE LIME FIZZ

Be sure all ingredients are chilled before you start,

and assemble just before serving.

Stir together 1 quart apple juice and 1/2 cup Rose's Lime Juice

in a pitcher. When ready to serve add 1 quart gingerale.

Stir gently. Garnish individual drinks with slices of lime or apple.

Ice cubes are not necessary if everything is very

cold to start with, but it's O.K. to serve

over ice cubes if desired. Serves 8

COCKTAILS FROM
SIX TO EIGHT

Angel Biscuits with Smithfield Ham   p34
Bluffton Artichoke Relish   p238
Meatballs Ellinghaus with Caper Sauce   p36

Orange Slices with Anchovies   p24
Christmasy Hush Puppies   p30

Swedish Herring Salad with Party Rye   p55
Baked Brie with Cranberry Chutney   p25
Baguette Rounds

Chocolate Truffles Grand Marnier   p244
White Chocolate Eggnog Fudge   p246

Zinfandel and Viognier

SAUCY JACK STONEY'S PLANTATION PUNCH

Combine 2 bottles Bacardi rum, and 4 cups freshly squeezed

grapefruit juice. Stir in enough Grenadine to color the punch

and suit your taste. Yields 12 powerful servings!

A HILTON HEAD
CHRISTMAS FEAST

Smoked Salmon in Endive Leaves   p24
Marvelous Mushroom Soup   p46

Roasted Mock Wild Boar with Sauce Grand Veneur   p80
Acorn Squash with Wild Rice and Pecans   p101
Cauliflower & Broccoli Dome   p105
Jeweled Cranberry Salad   p125

Steamed Persimmon Pudding with Rum Sauce   p144
Christmas Mints   p241

Morgan Zinfandel or Crôze Hermitage

AMBROSIA PUNCH

Combine 2 cups each chilled apricot nectar, orange juice, and

unsweetened pineapple juice in large pitcher. Stir in 1 (15-ounce) can

Coco Lopez cream and 1 1/2 cups light rum. Just before serving, place

block of ice in punch bowl. Add 1 (32-ounce) bottle club soda to juices

and pour slowly over ice. Serves 15

FIRESIDE SUPPER
FOR FAMILY & FRIENDS

Lowcountry Pickled Shrimp p16

Moussaka Mikanos p84
Green Salad with Greek Olives and Oregano

Danish Berry Pudding p161
Molasses Spice Cookies p203

Poor Man's Cinnamon Cake p153

Chateau Carras from Greece

SPICED CIDER WITH CALVADOS

Tie two broken cinnamon sticks and 1 tablespoon allspice berries in

cheese cloth. Place in non-reactive saucepan. Add 4 cups apple cider.

Heat slowly, but do not boil. Pour 1 ounce Calvados into each of 6

mugs. Add hot cider and stir with cinnamon stick. Serves 6

GOOD LUCK & PROSPERITY
A NEW YEAR'S EVE CELEBRATION

Four Sisters, Sauvignon Blanc

Terrine of Chicken Liver Paté in Aspic p33
Toasted Baguette Rounds
Christmas (or New Year's) Caviar Stars p22

Billi Billi Shiraz
Stags Leap Petite Syrah

Tourtière with Winter Chili Sauce p82
St. Helena Stew of Black-eyed Peas & Smoked Ham p78

New Year's Eve Caesar Salad p57
Cranberry Baked Alaska p130

Champagne

FESTIVE CHAMPAGNE PUNCH

Place small block of ice in punch bowl. In large pitcher mix 1 (750 ml)

bottle gin, 4 ounces sloe gin, and 1 quart gingerale. Add 1 bottle

champagne and slowly pour over block of ice.

Mix only one batch at a time. Have all ingredients chilled and do

not open gingerale or champagne until ready to mix.

Guaranteed to get any holiday party off to a festive start! Serves 12

THE HILTON HEAD
'EXCESSMAS'
HERBAL SOLUTION

If the holidays have been too much for you,
drink this potion based on a recipe found in an English herbal.
We added the Tabasco sauce for its reviving properties.

1 egg, pasteurized if desired
3 drops soy sauce
1 sage leaf, fresh, frozen or dried
1 drop, Tabasco sauce

Combine all ingredients in blender.
Blend well, drink slowly…
then
walk the beach, hit some balls, or hit the sack.

HAPPY NEW YEAR!

WINE & FOOD PAIRING REFERENCE

A summary of wines,   *suggested to accompany specific entrées.*

Pg.	Entrée	Wine selection
63	Wild Mushroom Ragù	Chianti Reserva / Pinot Grigio/Pinot Gris
64	Penne with Shrimp	Sangiovese / Italian B's / Gavi di Gavi
65	Salmon Oriental	W. Australian Chardonnay - Madfish
66	Shrimp 'n Grits	Chardonnay / light Zinfandel
67	Sea Bass en Papillote	Chardonnay - Chassagne Montrachet
68	Frogmore Stew	Beer / Languedoc - Corbières
69	Brunswick Stew (chicken/ham)	Gamay - Beaujolais
70	Sautéed Breasts of Chicken	Fumé Blanc - Ch. St. Jean, La Petite Etoile
71	Rock Cornish Hens	Merlot blend - Beringer Alluvium
72	Braised Quail	Pinot Grigio / Reisling
73	Duck with Mango Sauce	French Burgundy / Oregon Pinot Noir
74	Turkey Breast	Pinot Gris / Pinot Blanc
75	Roast Turkey	Sauvignon Blanc - J Fritz
76	Smithfield Ham Country-Style	Tavel Rosé / Rosé de Saignée
77	Glazed Baked Ham	Viognier - Condrieu or Beringer
78	Ham and Black-eyed Peas	Rhône - Domaine de la Renjarde / Petite Syrah - Stags Leap
79	Curried Loin of Pork Roast	S.Australian Shiraz - Richard Hamilton's Old Vines Reserve
80	Roast Mock Wild Boar	Zinfandel (full bodied)
82	Canadian Tourtière	S.E. Australia - Four Sisters, Sauv. Bl or Billi Billi, Shiraz/Cabernet
84	Moussaka Mikanos	Cabernet Sauvignon / Ch. Carras, Greece
85	Veal, Pork, Goulash	Gewurztraminer / Riesling Kabinet/Beer
86	Meatloaf with cheddar filling	Merlot (Chile) / Brunello (Italy)
87	Boeuf Bourguignon	Burgundy / Pinot Noir
88	Grilled Chuck Roast	Red Rhône (Crôzes-hermitage/Gigondas/Vacqueyras)
89	South-of-the-Broad Roast	Zinfandel - Chateau Souverain
90	Standing Rib Roast	Cabernet Sauvignon / Merlot Howard Park (Aust.)
92	Beef Tenderloin	Red Bordeaux / Cabernet Sauvignon
93	Rack of Lamb	Châteauneuf-du-Pape or Deakin Shiraz (Aust.)

The editors would like to share with you some interesting historic information and facts regarding our island of Hilton Head. Shaped like a boot, 13 miles long and 6 miles wide, this barrier island sits in the Atlantic ocean at the southern most point of South Carolina. Hilton Head anchors the base of the Lowcountry, which stretches up the coastal plain of the state from Georgia to the North Carolina border, and extends inland about 80 miles.

But it is the history of Hilton Head that breathes the life into what we have become today.

Discovered by the Spanish in 1521, the island had once been inhabited by nomadic tribes, some dating back to 2000 BC. Remnants of early encampments surrounded by shell rings up to 9 feet high and 240 feet across can be visited in Sea Pines Forest Preserve and off Squire Pope Road. Archaeological remains of native Americans and of Spanish settlements can still be found here.

In the 1560's French Huguenot colonists sought refuge on Hilton Head, fleeing persecution in their own Catholic homeland. They christened Port Royal Harbour, now known as Port Royal Sound, and charted the Island on French maps as 'Ile de la Rivière Grande'—Island of the Broad River. They soon moved to more protective waters, settling in the area known today as Beaufort.

English sea captain William Hilton landed on the Island in 1663. Commissioned by a group of Barbados planters to find new land to plant sugar and indigo, he was greeted by Spanish speaking Indians from the Yemassee tribe and the native Ewascus Indians. Captain Hilton soon claimed the Island for the British crown.

John Barnwell became our first settler in 1717, after receiving a grant of 500 acres in what is now Hilton Head Plantation. By 1860, 24 plantations were in operation on Hilton Head Island. Although the main crop was cotton, indigo, sugar cane, and rice were also cultivated.

Seven months after South Carolina seceded from the Union, shots fired on Fort Sumter reverberated on Hilton Head Island. On November 7, 1861, the Island became the scene of the largest naval battle fought in American waters. More than 12,000 Union soldiers and marines landed on the Island in less than five

hours. The Island fell into the hands of federal troops. At its peak, about 50,000 union soldiers occupied the Island, nearly twice the number of residents living here how.

With the Civil War and abolition of slavery, along with the boll weevil devastation of the cotton fields, Hilton Head lapsed into isolation for over 70 years.

The small population remaining were mostly descendants of former slaves. They farmed and relied on local waters for fish, shrimp, and oysters. Their culture and language, both known as Gullah, survive today as a living legacy of their strength and perseverance.

Until the 1950's, Hilton Head was a good place for timbering and deer hunting. One of the Island's largest tracts was owned by a Georgia family who decided that to get out of the timbering business and into land development. That first development—Sea Pines—was followed quickly by others: Shipyard, Palmetto Dunes, Wexford, Long Cove, Hilton Head Plantation, Spanish Wells, Indigo Run, Palmetto Hall Plantation, and Windmill Harbour.

Although incorporated as a town in 1983, simple times still prevailed.

Now, a mature resort island, with a tourist-based economy, the Island boasts world-class golf courses and tennis facilities with national championships, hotels, and award-winning restaurants. The New Year's Holiday brings an eclectic gathering of executives, judges, poets, authors, politicians, and media to a renowned retreat called Renaissance Weekend.

Over the years, great pains have been taken to preserve the Island's natural assets —its huge, spreading live oaks dripping with Spanish moss, its tall pines, its sandy beaches, its ocean, its creeks, channels, and marshes.

Despite rapid development in the past few years, parts of the Island remain as when sighted by Captain William Hilton's ship more than 300 years ago.

RECIPE CONTRIBUTORS

*Grateful acknowledgement to the good
cooks of Hilton Head Island who contributed recipes*

Joe Adams
Mary Lou Anton
Jean Applegate
Peggy Barton
Ann Beeler
Noel Berry
Lois Borders
Siv Borders
Jenese Busch
Katie Callahan
Betsy Catlin
Liz Cartwright
Madeline Cerrudo
Joanna Chase
Helen Cleary
Mary Lou Cost
Katherine Darragh
Rosemary Dean
Gerd Ericksson DeSalvio
Barbara Dill
Michelle Drago
Dottie Dunbar
Lilian Ellinghaus
Helen Fairchild
Edna Felix
Nita Furner
Trudy Frantz
Barbara Gaebe
Peggy Gail
Terry Gebhardt
Mary Ann Goodrich
Diane Gren
Pamela Hanlin

Jean Harney
Judy Harrison
Pat Haskell
Maryjean Herberger
Nancy Hewitt
Bette Herbig
Jan Hilton
Virginia Jordan
Betsy Jukofsky
Elizabeth Kent
Joanne Lockemer
Betty Jane Luke
Darcy Lukemeyer
Barb Lothrop
Nancy Laterza
Fran Langenhan
Lauren Marlis
Susan Marshall
Gladys Mendschine
Pat Moore
Jillian Murray
Katherine Murray
Lea Murray
Lindsay Murray
Tina Novit
Wayne L. Oakes
Inga Owen
Sue O'Sullivan
Cheryl Pearce
Johnee Pinckney
Jane Plante
Lois Plekenpol
Jean Posselius

Christine Rahn
Jane Rawlings
Dori Reichardt
Pat Sanderson
Pete Scarfaro
Ivy Smith
Peggy Smith
Joan Stafford
Betty Stein
B.J. Studebaker
Marion Sullivan
Barbara Swift
Peg Tambke
Cindy Tuttle
June Vercellotti
Patricia Walter
Allein Ward
Charlotte Ward
Pat Walzel
Evelyn Wavpotich
Jane Weidenbacher
Mary Lou Werner
Marilyn Whitton
Elaine Wilcox
Mary Lou Wilhelm
Pat Williams
Irene Williamson
Dixie Wink
Stell Wood
Lori Zudell
Ben Zudell
Alex Zudell

INDEX

INDEX

INDEX

INDEX

NDEX

INDEX

NDEX

INDEX

INDEX

NDEX

INDEX

INDEX

TO ORDER
Yuletide on Hilton Head

Indicate number of copies _____ @ $19.95 (U.S.) each = _____
plus postage/handling @ $4.00 each = _____
add sales tax (for delivery if in S.C.) @ $1.20 each = _____
Check or Credit Card *(Canada - credit card only, please)* Total = _____

Charge to my: ☐ Visa ☐ Mastercard

Account #:

Expires on: (mo/yr)

Signature _____
(Required if using charge card)
NAME _____
STREET _____
CITY_____STATE _____ ZIP _____

MAIL TO:

P.O. Box 22961
Hilton Head Island
SC 29925

All copies will be sent to same address unless otherwise specified. If you wish one or any number of books sent as gifts, furnish a list of names and addresses of recipients. If you wish to enclose your own gift card with each book, please write name of recipient on outside of your envelope, enclose with order, and we will include it with your gift.

TO ORDER
Yuletide on Hilton Head

Indicate number of copies _____ @ $19.95 (U.S.) each = _____
plus postage/handling @ $4.00 each = _____
add sales tax (for delivery if in S.C.) @ $1.20 each = _____
Check or Credit Card *(Canada - credit card only, please)* Total = _____

Charge to my: ☐ Visa ☐ Mastercard

Account #:

Expires on: (mo/yr)

Signature _____
(Required if using charge card)
NAME _____
STREET _____
CITY_____STATE _____ ZIP _____

MAIL TO:

P.O. Box 22961
Hilton Head Island
SC 29925

All copies will be sent to same address unless otherwise specified. If you wish one or any number of books sent as gifts, furnish a list of names and addresses of recipients. If you wish to enclose your own gift card with each book, please write name of recipient on outside of your envelope, enclose with order, and we will include it with your gift.